# Journey through

# The Living Deserts

# of

# South Africa

by

## CM Dean

Published by
Dean & Associates Ltd.
16 Swallow Dale, Thringstone, Coalville, Leics.
LE67 8LY  England
Tel/Fax:  +44 (0)1530 222 799
Email:  DeanAssocsLtd@aol.com

# Map and Setion References

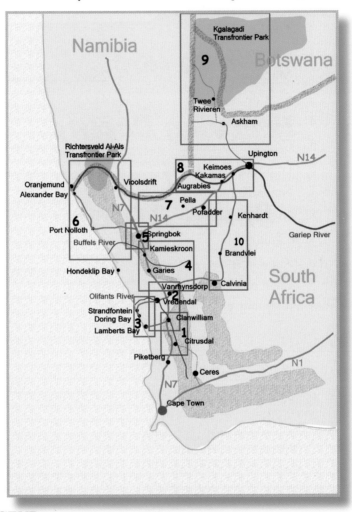

## LEGEND

| | |
|---|---|
| National borders | National roads |
| Rivers | Secondary tarred roads |
| Parks and Reserves | Secondary untarred |
| Mountains | Farm tracks |
| | **4x4** 4x4 trails |

| | |
|---|---|
| ◇ | Diamonds |
| ⊛ | Flowers |
| 🚶 | Hiking trails |
| **M** | Historical monuments |
| 🍷 | Wine cellars |

# Table of Contents

# Special Inserts

# Timeline of the north-western Cape

| | People and Politics | Mineral Wealth | Heritage and Conservation |
|---|---|---|---|
| 10,000-0 BC | San roamed freely throughout Southern Africa. | | San rock art in caves. |
| 0-1650 | Khoikhoi moved south and competes with San nomads for food and land. | Khoikhoi discovered copper in the mountains around Springbok. | |
| 1650-1800 | 1652 The Dutch established a halfway station at the Cape. They explored the western coast to Springbok. Migrant farmers moved along the coast resulting in wars with the Khoisan and settlements along the Olifants River. | 1685 Copper found by Simon van der Stel at Springbok but not in economically viable amounts. | |
| 1800-1850 | 1806 The British occupation of the Cape. Missionary societies moved into the area. | | 1806 Cederberg conservation control started by JF Budler. |
| 1850-1900 | Expansion of Missionary Society work in the area. 1890s Settlement of impoverished farmers near Kakamas. Development of the Gariep irrigation scheme. | 1852 First commercial copper mine started at Springbok. Development of Okiep and Nababeep as copper mining towns. | |
| 1900-1950 | 1901 - 1902 The Anglo Boer War reached the western Cape. 1920s The Olifants River irrigation scheme was developed. 1920s and 1930s Fish and crayfish canning factories were built in coastal villages. | Slump and recovery of the copper market. 1925 The discovery of diamonds along the coast and declaration of restricted zones. 1940 Iron ore at Sishen resulted in the railway line past Lutzville in the 1970s. | 1929 Sir Malcolm Campbell attempted a land speed record at Verneukpan. 1931 Kalahari Gemsbok Park proclaimed. |
| 1950-1994 | 1950 Group Areas Act resulted in the marginalisation of ethnic groups and the closure of some mission stations. | 1970 Started off-shore diamond mining through dredging of the sea bed. | 1966 Augrabies National Park created. 1973 Cederberg Wilderness Area proclaimed. |
| 1994-today | Redistribution of wealth through the provision of basic facilities to all and the sharing of initiatives and projects to promote the regions. | Slowing down of diamond activities | 1999 Kgalagadi Transfrontier Park with Botswana. 2003 Richtersveld/Ai-Ais Transfrontier Park signed withNamibia. Local parks and initiatives. |

# The Dream

'I can only imagine one thing better than this!' The comment floated lazily in the air for a few moments, waiting for a challenge. The six of us just finished a great barbecue and were enjoying a relaxing summer evening on Johanna's patio.

'Carry on,' said Johan.

'To be sitting around a camp fire in the Kalahari, listen to the sounds of the desert and marvel at the night sky.'

The tone of the conversation changed, slowly at first and then with increasing enthusiasm as we remembered days gone by, places visited and the yearning for the places still on the 'to be seen' list. Johan, Johanna and I were born in Namaqualand and Johanna still lives there. This made it easier for Johan and his wife Janey, and Dave and myself to return with our families over the years. Paul, Dave's brother and the sixth member of the group was the only newcomer to the area.

'Well, what is stopping us?' asked Dave. 'We have all retired, time is no problem and it's possible to visit all these places within a budget to suit our pockets, if we plan it properly!'

That was the moment when the dream became reality. The six of us would go on a tour through the north-western Cape region of South Africa where you can still become one with nature. We would revisit all the old familiar sites and add all the ones we always wanted to see, but this time with a difference. It will not be a visit to tourist sites alone, but a journey of discovery and understanding - why are the places there, what happened in the past and what do they have to offer all year round.

This book follows the actual tour from the Cederberg to the Kgalagadi Transfrontier Park and back. The thin story line allows personal impressions, photographs are included for clarity, and the chapter on Practical Touring at the end can help other travellers to plan and enjoy similar tours.

Each chapter starts off with a map of the area covered in the chapter and the key contacts for further information. Information blocks can provide quick summaries on towns and villages covered. Note however that the maps are not to scale or comprehensive and should not be relied on without official maps.

Do come with us on our journey of discovery through these living deserts of South Africa.

# 1. Cederberg

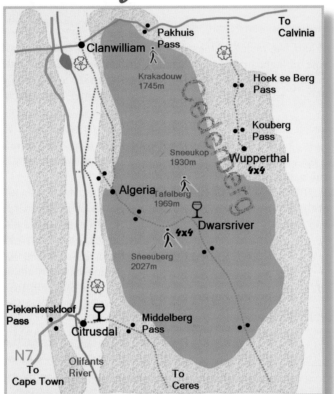

**West Coast Regional Tourism Organisation**
PO Box 242, Moorreesburg 7310
Tel: +27 (0)22 433 2380
Email: tourism@capewestcoast.org
Website: www.capewestcoast.org

**Citrusdal Tourism Bureau**
39 Voortrekker Street, PO Box 425
Citrusdal 7340
Tel: +27 (0)22 921 3210

**Clanwilliam Tourism Bureau**
Main Road, PO Box 5
Clanwilliam 8135
Tel. +27 (0)27 482 2024

**Western Cape Nature Conservation Board**
Private Bag X100, Cape Town 8000
Tel: +27 (0)21 483 4615
Email: Cederberg@cnc.org.za
Website: www.capenature.org.za

**Cederberg Wilderness Area**
PO Box 6, Porterville 6810
Tel +27 (0)22 931 2088

**Wupperthal Tourism Bureau**
Church Square, Wupperthal
Tel: +27 (0)27 492 3410

# 1. Cederberg

## Piekenierskloof pass

Piekenierskloof, the ravine of the pikemen. A suitable springboard for our tour. We stop at the lay-by on the N7 near the top of Piekenierskloof pass and survey the scenery below. In the distance a hazy Table Mountain forms a blip on the horizon, offset by the brown, green and yellow mosaic of the Swartland or black country, the bread basket of the Cape. Across the plain, Piketberg, the most northerly town of the Swartland, nestles at the foot of a mountain with the same name. During the winter or spring the colours will change to a more soothing green, but as we chose summer for the tour, we are satisfied with the brown. It has been easy going from Cape Town to this point, with no mountains obstructing the way, but this is about to change as we cross the first of the mountain ranges stretching all the way along the western coast of South Africa.

The Dutch explored this part of the country during the latter part of the 17th century, found nothing except some copper in inaccessible locations, and left. The British made some attempt to introduce Irish settlers to Clanwilliam during the 1820s, failed and left the area alone. What is therefore awaiting us is a part of South Africa that was allowed to develop its own culture along the early Khoisan and Dutch styles, unburdened by external influences.

You have to go back at least 300 years, to the time of the Dutch settlement in the Cape in 1652, to find the origin of the current name. The Dutch East India Company (VOC) was never really interested in the colonisation of Africa. Their only objective was to establish a half-way station where they could obtain fresh provisions for their ships en route to the East Indian Islands. The expansion towards permanent settlement was evolutionary, rather than planned, spearheaded by the company's effort to make the outpost self-sufficient. A small number of employees were allowed to lease farms as free burghers in 1657, and although the original directives from the company were to keep the peace and only to trade with the local Khoikhoi tribes, expansion led to tension.

The Dutch encountered two different groups of indigenous peoples at the Cape, the San and the Khoikhoi. The San consisted of small nomadic family groups living off the land and hunting animals for food, thus incurring the name of Bushmen from the Dutch. They were the original inhabitants, widely found throughout Southern Africa as early as 10,000 years ago. Around 2,000 years ago the Khoikhoi also moved south from Botswana. Because of the similar click sounding language, the San and Khoikhoi are often referred to as the Khoisan. One

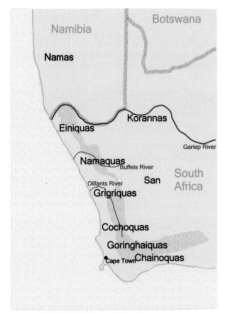

*Above: Distribution of the Khoikhoi tribes along the western Cape during the 1600s*

theory is that they are related, but that the Khoikhoi learnt to become herdsmen from other African tribes in Botswana, and grew taller because of their better diet and more settled lifestyle. Khoikhoi, or 'men of men' as they called themselves, lived a hierarchical tribal structure. One tribe may consist of a few smaller family groups being loyal to the tribal chief. They measured their wealth in the size of the communal tribal herd, and although they were trading cattle with the Dutch, they were not averse to raids against neighbouring tribes or even the Dutch farmers, to replenish these trading losses.

During the mid 1600s, the main Khoikhoi tribes were the Goringhaiquas and Chainoquas near the Cape, the Cochoquas further north, and the Grigriquas, Namaquas and Namas along the western coast of South Africa. After the first rebellion by the Goringhaiquas, under Doman, against the encroaching settlements on their land in 1659, the nearby tribes were forced to accept a peace treaty with the Dutch in exchange for trade and protection. This promise of protection led directly to further skirmishes between the Dutch and non-aligned Khoikhoi tribes, and the naming of Piekenierskloof.

Cochoquas under the chieftainship of Gonnema were by far the richest tribe in the Cape and indulged in frequent cattle raids on other smaller tribes to maintain and increase this wealth. In 1675 a party of musketeers and pikemen (horse and footmen) were sent from the Cape to protect allied tribes against cattle raids near Piketberg. The campaign was successful in reclaiming the cattle but Gonnema's men fled over the pass to the frustration of the pikemen, unable to transport their heavy pikes in pursuit. They were however immortalised by having the pass over the mountains named after them, replacing the original name of Groote Cloof, meaning large ravine.

A smallpox epidemic in the Cape in 1713 devastated the Khoikhoi tribes around the Cape and the Cochoquas, Goringhaiquas and Chainoquas became collectively known as Hottentots. This name, although later used in a derogatory sense, actually dates back to 1620 when Augustin de Beaulieu stated that, in their clicking language, the Khoikhoi greeting sounded like 'hautitou'. Northerly tribes like the Namaquas, Grigriquas and Namas however retained their identities.

Like all European explorers, the Dutch did have one additional ambition when they settled at the Cape, namely to search for and find Monomotapa, the legendary land of riches. Based on distorted accounts of tribal myths by the earliest explorers to Africa, Monomotapa was supposed to be an empire in the African interior, with Vigiti Magna as its capital, and a treasure city called Davagul. Maps around the 16th century even indicated the possible location of Monomotapa! Explorations subsidised by the VOC started early and were well documented, including crossings at Piekenierskloof which was introduced to the explorers by their Khoi guides in 1660. Dankaert, the leader of one of the expeditions, described an incident in his diary when his party met local Khoikhoi men in the ravine who have never before seen white men. The Khoikhoi caught such a fright that they fled, leaving behind their provisions of roasted dassie and honey, to the delight of the guides who laid claim to the booty! This was however the only treasure they found and the explorers returned empty-handed to the Cape.

Piekenierskloof, although treacherous, became the accepted gateway to the north-west by the late 18th century. Thomas Bain, one of the greatest pass-builders in South African history, rebuilt the pass during the late 1850s and renamed it Grey's pass in honour of the resident governor of the Cape, Sir George Grey. It was only after the final reconstruction of the pass in the 1950s that the name reverted back to Piekenierskloof pass.

But we must move on. Once you cross the pass you are in a different world. Gone is the hustle and bustle of the cities and the popular tourist spots and you know you can enjoy your visit in a more relaxed atmosphere.

## Olifants River Valley

I cannot help the feeling of excitement at each first glimpse of the Olifants River valley from the top of Piekenierskloof. The evergreen citrus groves and the changing colour of the wheat fields along the banks of the river contrast well with the fynbos on the slopes of the nearby hills and the ragged blue backdrop of the Cederberg mountains. The Olifants River is one of the few perennial rivers in South Africa. Known to the Khoikhoi as the Tharakamma or the rough overgrown river, it was renamed the Olifants River by early explorers after a herd of around 300 elephants was spotted in the valley. None of the elephants survived, most of the overgrowth disappeared and, after the final skirmish in the Olifants River valley in 1739, the remaining Khoikhoi were forced to submit as labourers on farms, settle on mission stations, or move further north. Migrant farmers settled in the valley and the fertile wilderness became prosperous and cultivated.

The road to Citrusdal leaves the N7 at the foot of the Piekenierskloof pass but we have to make two detours.

The first stop at the **Craig Royston** farm is quite close to the turn-off. Craig Royston, the owner of this early farm, started a trading outpost on his farm and for years held the right of trader, post office and even hotelier in the area. During the 1860s, on the recommendation of Thomas Bain, the low-water crossing over the river was replaced by a bridge to meet up with the newly constructed Grey's pass and the popularity of the Royston farm declined in favour of Citrusdal, which developed around the new river crossing.

The original trading post with its green corrugated iron roof is still there with the hotel building behind it, now a farm house. Inside the shop, trading is also still brisk, but this time for the Olifants River wine cellars and other local produce. This is an excellent place to get a preview of the wines we can expect on our wine route stops, and we

stock up on buchu brandy, complete with sprigs of the buchu plant in the bottle. It is interesting that distilling used to be as popular as wine production in the region of the Olifants River. At the peak of the distillation craze during the late 19th century, distilling permits were handed out so lavishly that one farmer even received a licence to distil the produce of a single vine! Most popular products for distillation were and still are brandy and witblits. Witblits or white lightning, is distilled from the sweet white hanepoot grape to a spirit upwards of 66 percent proof and is favoured by the strong and the brave as a cure for everything from flu to toothache.

Our second stop is at **The Baths,** a detour of 12 km further along the foot of the mountain. Known for centuries to the Khoisan for its healing powers, the spring water is lukewarm, contains no dissolved gasses or unusual mineral salts, but has at 14.8 Mach units, a slightly higher level of radio-activity, thus indicating a journey through some radioactive substrata. It is completely safe and drinkable. The resort offers one cold pool, one warm pool and a few in-house jacuzzis, as well as self-catering and camping accommodation, with extensive improvements in progress. Hiking trails around the resort bring you in close contact with the numerous bird species spotted in the area.

We stop at the well-stocked shop and are joined by one of the managers for the fascinating story of the property. The first mention of The Baths dates back to 1739 when the site formed one of two military

---

## Citrusdal

All business facilities
Hotels, full range of accommodation
Restaurants

**Attractions:**
Historical buildings and museums
Craig Royston and The Baths
Wine cellar
Citrus Fruit Co-operative
Hiking and 4x4 trails

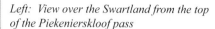

*Left: View over the Swartland from the top of the Piekenierskloof pass*

*Below left: The original Craig Royston trading store*

*Below: Sandveldhuisie in Citrusdal*

outposts erected along the Olifants River to quell the unrest caused by illegal bartering, theft and counter-theft of cattle among the white settlers and the Khoikhoi tribes. Since that date, to the mid 19th century, The Baths were in the hands of the Cape Government. Depending on the local fashion, it was either frequented by affluent residents from the Cape, or left to deteriorate.

In 1856 the location was first sold to private owners and often changed hands until 1903, when it was bought by James McGregor. James was a Scotsman who fell in love with the area and a local girl, Lenie van Wyk. He made a promise never to take her to his foreign country, and the purchase of The Baths at an auction was one way to prove his intention of keeping his promise. After 100 years the farm is still in the hands of the McGregor family, and increasing in popularity as a resort.

## Citrusdal

Citrusdal, our main stop for the day, is a thriving town and the centre of the Cape citrus region. We are keen to see what Citrusdal has to offer in addition to the standard sporting and action facilities such as golf, canoeing or drives, but only after a chance to cool off in the hotel. Citrusdal, situated low in the valley and surrounded by high mountains, can be hot in summer and it is mid-afternoon before we feel ready to explore the town. With the wine cellars in the town and near the Goede

Hoop citrus packing store, the tour turns out to be effortless and pleasurable. Wines have only been produced by the Citrusdal Cooperative Wine Cellars since 1958, but wine production in the region dates back more than two centuries. For that matter, Napoleon requested a sweet wine from the farm Brakfontein near Citrusdal as a companion during his period of exile on St. Helena! The Citrusdal wines cover the full South African range, made from grapes grown over a wide geographic as well as climatic regions, including grapes grown under dry-land conditions.

The Goede Hoop Citrus Cooperative on the other hand, presents a different perspective on agriculture in the valley. It is one of the largest citrus packing sheds in South Africa, and packs approximately 30 percent of the country's export navel oranges. Like the vineyards, oranges have been cultivated in the valley for over two centuries. Living proof of this is the oldest orange tree in South Africa, growing on the farm Heksrivier (witch river), and purported to be over 200 years old. The tree burnt down in 1925 but sprouted again, is still bearing fruit,

and was recently declared a national monument.

The next morning before leaving Citrusdal, we spend an interesting couple of hours in the museum and the Sandveldhuisie. The original church building was given a new lease of life as the local museum, filled with photos, farming implements and information about the history of the region. It is however the Sandveldhuisie, a typical thatched roof cottage built by the early settlers, which really takes our fancy. Packed with all kinds of local produce, arts and crafts, we spend some time deciding what to buy as souvenirs and titbits for the rest of the tour.

## Cederberg Wilderness Area

The N7 snakes alongside the Olifants River as we pass orange groves, roadside shops and the turn-off towards Algeria. This revives vivid memories of the Cederberg Wilderness Area for us. As a junior teacher I spent an invigorating weekend with the school's mountaineering club climbing Wolfberg and abseiling down the Wolfberg Arch, but it was the week we spent with our young families in two of the chalets in the park that are foremost in our minds. During that magical week we made excursions to the stadsaalgrotte or town hall caves, went on hikes (and tiptoeing around a snake curled up in the footpath), swam in the local dam and climbed Wolfberg. Well actually,

---

**Cederberg Wilderness Area**
Limited business facilities
Guest houses, self catering, camping

**Attractions:**
Mountaineering
Hiking
4x4 trails
Mountain biking

---

*Above left: Rock formations in the Cederberg mountains near the Pakhuis pass*

*Above right: Road from Citrusdal to Ceres through the Cederberg mountains*

Johan and I climbed Wolfberg with his teenage sons, while Janey, Dave and Johanna suddenly realised that someone had to look after the other youngsters - a lame excuse as the owner of the farm said that even a five year old child could climb the mountain! I have to admit that it could only have been a local fit five year old, and our two city born-and-bred children were not keen to prove him right or wrong.

The Cederberg range got its name from the wild indigenous cedar trees (Widdringtonia cedarbergensis) which covered the mountains until two centuries ago. Indiscriminate felling for household use and as telephone poles, and excessive burning of the fynbos in the mountains reduced their numbers to a few, hidden in ravines or amongst boulders. Although attempts were made towards conservation ever since the appointment of JF Budler as the first forest ranger in 1876, the early policies favoured a multi-purpose management of forest resources. This included the selling of dry wood from the trees and the harvesting of rooibos and buchu, thus causing more harm than good. Fortunately the remaining trees and shrubs are today fully protected within the boundaries of the Cederberg Wilderness Area, proclaimed in 1973, and carefully managed to ensure the survival of the various indigenous species.

**Algeria**, near the entrance of the Cederberg Wilderness Area, is 30 km along a dirt road from the N7. The Wilderness Area extends over 71,000 ha from north of the Pakhuis pass near Clanwilliam, to Citrusdal and operates a practical permit system to balance the needs for conservation with the demands of tourism and leisure activities in the area. The reserve is divided into three separate sectors and only a certain maximum number of hikers or visitors with valid permits are allowed to drive, hike or camp in each sector at one time. Strict rules apply to where you may camp or picnic, but otherwise hikers can wander around freely within their allocated sector if in possession of a suitable map. This allows them to view the wind sculptured

*Above: Rooibos tea shrubs in the Cederberg region*

*Above right: Rooibos Ltd head office building in Clanwilliam*

rocks such as the Maltese Cross and the Wolfberg Arch, and the unique flora like the fynbos, rooibos and buchu plants at leisure. For the less energetic visitors, like us, the town hall caves are within driving reach and the park offers excellent well-marked walks around the accommodation or parking spots.

There are also quite a few guest farms around the park, from which you can venture into the reserve by car. One of the interesting farms is Dwarsrivier where the Nieuwoudt family specialises in high altitude vineyards. It is a private cellar who started producing their award-winning wines in 1977 and claims to produce wines from the highest vineyards in South Africa.

## Fynbos, rooibos and buchu

As one of the major plant kingdoms, 6,000 of the 8,500 known varieties of the fynbos biome are found in South Africa, mainly around the Cape Peninsula and in the Cederberg range. Most common are the grey leaf sugar bush (Protea laurifolia) at low altitudes, the Catherine wheel pincushion protea (Leucospermum catherinse) along streams, and various ericas along the drier rocky slopes. Unique to the highest peaks in the Cederberg range like Sneeuberg 2,028 m, Tafelberg 1,971 m, Sneeukop 1,932 m, and Krakadouw 1,737 m, is the snow protea (Protea cryophila). During winter this plant is covered by snow and flowers directly from a narrow strip stem which often grows in cracks or underground as protection against the freezing winters and scorching temperatures in summer. It takes about a year for the flower to open fully, but then it is an exceptional flower. Shaped like the well known king protea (Protea cynaroides) it is up to 160 mm in diameter with a snow white fluffy centre surrounded by crimson petals. Finding one, seemingly sprouting directly from the soil, or even better as a bright red flower against the snow in winter is a real treat.

Rooibos (Aspalathus linearis), or red bush, has become a real ambassador for its region of origin. It is a bush with leaves like needles which, if harvested and treated (chopped, bruised, fermented and dried), can be brewed into a pleasant tasting tea, containing no caffeine, very low tannin and with a potent antioxidant effect. It has been used over the centuries as a cure for colic, allergies and other ailments, and I can vouch that once you get hooked on the taste, it is difficult to switch back to other teas. It became known outside the area once Dr. P Nortier and others managed to cultivate the bush commercially in the 1930s and is now on sale world wide in health shops and on the shelves of supermarkets. Building on its anti-allergenic characteristics, other products like hand creams, shampoos and conditioners are also marketed by Rooibos Limited in Clanwilliam.

Buchu (Agathosma betulina) is another medicinal herb unique to the Cederberg area. The plant has a rubbery leaf with tiny pockets of oil, collected at the end of the growing season and used locally as a herbal drink or flavouring. It has a distinctive fruity, minty aroma and is frequently used to flavour food, drinks or medicine, like the buchu brandy we bought at Craig Royston. During the early 20th century it was also used as a remedy for bladder and kidney problems.

## Clanwilliam

After the Algeria turn-off, the N7 moves away from the river and over some hills. We join the river again at the top end of the Clanwilliam Dam, the backbone of the Olifants River irrigation scheme. Our destination is Clanwilliam, one of the few towns on our route moulded by the early history along the river, and then frozen in time.

The first two explorations during the time of Jan van Riebeeck in the 1660s, both reached the Olifants River near the current location of Clanwilliam where the Jan Dissels River joins the Olifants River. It was only later that the easier route along the coastal Sandveld was taken. The first recorded farm in the area dates back to 1725 and soon a village developed, called Jan Disselsvalleij, the valley of Jan Dissels, destined to become one of the ten oldest towns in South Africa. The early road along the Olifants River crossed the river at this spot, and the town prospered to such an extent that it was earmarked as a new district in 1803. In 1814 Sir John Cradock, the resident governor

---

### Clanwilliam

All business facilities
Hotels, full range of accommodation
Restaurants

**Attractions:**
Historical buildings and museums
Rooibos tea and velskoen factories
Clanwilliam Dam and water sport
Ramskop Nature Reserve, flowers
San rock art and hiking

---

at the Cape, renamed the town after his father-in-law, the Earl of Clanwilliam and awarded it full magisterial power. On the maps of the 1820s the district of Clanwilliam covered the whole area from the Olifants River valley to the Buffels River near Springbok. When the system of divisional councils was introduced in 1855, Clanwilliam was thus the logical choice as the seat for the Namaqualand region.

After British colonisation of the Cape in 1806, their growing concern became the unrest along the eastern borders of the colony. To alleviate this problem the Cape Government arranged for British immigrants to boost the white population in the Cape along these borders in 1820, but a group of Irish immigrants was also sent to Clanwilliam. This arrangement was not very successful, due to the high temperatures of over 40 degrees Centigrade in summer. Only six families eventually stayed on. Thomas Birt Bayly was the first to be buried in the church yard of Anglican Church in 1842, but it was the Fryer family who would play a significant role. Richard Fryer became the owner of the farm, Hollebaksfontein, on which Strandfontein later developed on the coast, and Charles Fryer became the first mayor when Clanwilliam achieved municipal status in 1901.

However, Clanwilliam district was too large to be administered effectively and in 1892 it was subdivided into six smaller districts. Clanwilliam's influence was shrinking in favour of Vanrhynsdorp, Springbok and other district councils.

The final straws were the development of the Olifants River irrigation scheme during the 1920s, the construction of the railway line along the Sandveld and the eventual relocation of the N7 main road to the western bank of the Olifants River. Clanwilliam became isolated and lost its dominant position.

Clanwilliam justifiably capitalises on its history. The main street is concrete as tar can melt in the high summer temperatures, and is lined with historic buildings. The old Drostdy built in 1808, for instance, used to be the first magistrate's court and residence with two rooms added as the local jail. These rooms had no windows and the air used to become so stale that prisoners regularly had to be handcuffed and let out into the street to allow the rooms, and themselves, to be aired. In 1877 a new prison was built which was eventually sold to the local Nature Conservation and Development Society as a museum. It houses a large collection of local memorabilia collected by Rheinholdt Strassberger over a period of time.

The name Strassberger is a reminder of one of the main reasons why Dave insisted that we include Clanwilliam as a key stop-over on the tour. For years he has been a fan of the Strassberger velskoene. Velskoene, literally translating into skin or field shoes, are typical from the Cederberg region and very popular with local farmers and hikers. Today we are stopping at the factory so that he can pick up two pairs of golf shoes they have made for his golfing friends, and the rest

*Above left: Ramskop Nature Reserve near Clanwilliam*

*Above right: Inside the Strassberger's Shoe factory in Clanwilliam*

*Left: Clanwilliam historic magistrate's offices and jail*

of us can admire the shoes and shirts on offer.

In 1904 the Rev. Willy Strassberger was sent by the Rhenish Missionary Society to Wupperthal to assist the Reverend Schmolke in his work. With his banking background, Strassberger realised the value of the shoe factory already operational in Wupperthal and convinced the Society to continue their support for it, despite the remoteness of the site. After retirement the Reverend Strassberger and his son Heinie opened their own factory in Clanwilliam in 1941, based on the same principles as the factory in Wupperthal. They actively marketed their products and never looked back. Today the Strassberger's Hotel in the main street also belongs to one of the Strassberger Brothers and is an

excellent place to stay with its swimming pool offering welcome relief on the hot summer days, and a restaurant renowned for its cuisine.

Since the Rooibos Tea Company head office is close to the shoe factory, we decide to pay it an impromptu visit. The staff are very accommodating. They answer all our questions on the history of the industry and have various brochures, recipe books and products for us to try.

At the hotel Dave heads for the pool while the rest of us explore the town, our first stop being the well stocked and professional information centre in the old church hall. A gentle walk along the main street brings us to the historical buildings such as the jail opposite the information centre, the restored period house dating back to the 1920s opposite the hotel, now containing craft shops and a tea room, and the old Dutch Reformed Church, built in 1864. This church is also known as the Flower Church as it becomes the centre of a wild flower show during August and September each year.

The Anglican Church, built in 1867, was designed by Sophie Gray, the wife of Dr. Robert Gray who was sent to the Cape as the first Anglican bishop with the remit to establish the Anglican faith in South Africa. Sophie designed most of the Anglican churches built during the second half of the 19th century in South Africa. It is in this church yard where we are able to trace the history of the English settlers in town.

Clanwilliam boasts a few more recent famous residents including C. Louis Leipoldt and Tolla van der Merwe. C. Louis Leipoldt, paediatrician, poet of national standing, author and chef, was the grandson of a Wupperthal missionary and the house where he used to live is on the main street of Clanwilliam. His love for this part of the Cape shone through his poems and after his death in 1947 he was granted his wish to be buried next to the Pakhuis pass between Clanwilliam and Wupperthal. Tolla van der Merwe, a local resident and well known national story-teller and comedian was born in Clanwilliam in 1943 and was also buried there after his untimely death in a car accident in 2000. His talent is still widely missed.

Before sunset we take a short trip to the Ramskop Nature Reserve and the Clanwilliam Dam. It is not the best time of the year to visit the wild flower garden in the nature reserve as this part of the park really has to be experienced during the flower season from August to September. The succulents, indigenous quiver trees and aloes however, prove to be worthy substitutes any time of the year.

The Clanwilliam dam on the other hand could have offered a holiday in its own right. Built as part of the Olifants River irrigation scheme, it not only ensures a constant flow of water to the vineyards and other irrigation small holdings downstream of the dam, but offers excellent leisure facilities like sailing, water skiing and angling. The dam contains quite a few indigenous fish species such as the Clanwilliam redfin or catfish, both unfortunately on the endangered or vulnerable list. The annual Bass Classic angling tournament is very popular and attracts anglers from all over South Africa.

At the end of a packed day we are ready to sample the delights of the local cuisine and a well-deserved rest.

## Rock Paintings

Have you ever looked at a mountain and thought 'I can get lost here and still love every minute of it'? This is how I feel at the top of the Pakhuis pass. The

*Above left: The dancing women San paintings on the Sevilla trail*

*Above right: Animals and hunting scenes in San rock paintings*

wind-shaped rocks are stacked like heaps of broken bricks on a disused building site, or boxes in a warehouse, untidily stacked on top of each other.

For that matter, 'warehouse' is one of the explanations for the name Pakhuis, although there is another school of thought linking the name to a Khoikhoi word meaning 'the rocky place of the dassies'. The pass itself was also built by Thomas Bain, who constructed the Piekenierskloof pass, after Clanwilliam petitioned for a link to the upper Karoo and Calvinia. The pass was completed in 1877. Bain was reported to be very fond of the mountains and used to explore the area on horseback to discover rock paintings.

Having left Clanwilliam early in the morning on the way to Wupperthal, we stop to pay homage to Leipoldt at his grave. The grave is in a secluded spot under an overhang and it is obvious why he loved this part and wanted to be buried here on top of the pass. He even personally named the three peaks opposite his grave

Faith, Hope and Charity. From the top we can see the plain where we hope to find some of the San rock paintings so numerous in this region.

We stop at Traveller's Rest farm, pick up a permit and map for the rock paintings from the farm house, and follow the easy level footpath next to the Brandewyn River, causing some speculation as to the whereabouts of the paintings. You usually associate rock paintings with the presence of large overhangs or boulders, and as far as we can see, there is no sign of any. However after a while the boulders start to show along the banks of the river and we are spoilt for choice to photograph the ten available sites of rock paintings. Most of the sites contain the usual animals and hunters you would expect from San rock paintings, but three stand out. The one site shows a group of dancing women and the second site several processions. But it is the low overhanging rock which apparently was used as a kraal in the past and displays handprints, also from children, that is really interesting - not

19

your professional San painter at work. Some experts even claim that handprints are not genuine San artwork, but were made by Khoikhoi children!

We continue on our way to Wupperthal, passing the turn-off to the Bushman's Kloof Wilderness Reserve, developed as a luxury game lodge and reserve. To the left is another turn-off towards Klawer and Elizabethfontein on which is a primary school of note. This school is not only one of the largest farm schools, but its Betjesfontein Dance Group has performed local dances to wide audiences. Visitors are welcome to watch the dances by appointment with the principal.

Just before the turn-off to Wupperthal is a signpost towards the Englishman's grave. Lieut. Graham Clowes from the First Battalion of the Gordon Highlanders, was killed in January 1901 while scouting during the Anglo Boer War, and was buried on site. His mother came from Hertfordshire to erect a memorial stone and continued to visit the grave for many years.

The road to Wupperthal from this turn-off is an experience. You have to go over two very steep and narrow mountain passes. The first pass takes us into the Biedouw valley and then there is another pass over the Kouberg to Wupperthal. Both passes, though in good condition, are very steep and the worst parts have concrete strips in the centre to assist traction in wet weather. The views over the two enclosed valleys are impressive and make up for the nail-biting sections of the passes.

Like Pakhuis, the name Biedouw has more than one explanation of origin. One group links the name to the daisy Tripteris oppositifolia, known as 'bietou' in the area, but a more authentic explanation links it to the poisonous milk bush, Euphorbia mauritanica, which is found in abundance along the road from the valley to Calvinia, and known to the Khoikhoi as 'bie' or 'wie'. Kouberg on the other hand is a combination of a Khoi word meaning last, and the Dutch word for mountain, and as we stop at the top to look down into the Wupperthal valley, we can understand the relief of the early residents in crossing this last mountain!

## Wupperthal

Basic business facilities
Self catering and camping

**Attractions:**
Historical buildings
Rooibos tea and shoe factories
Hiking, 4x4 trails
Flowers in spring

## Wupperthal

In 1830 the Reverends Johan Gottlieb Leipoldt and Baron Theobold von Wurmb established one of the oldest Rhenish mission stations in the Western Cape at Wupperthal. It was said that

*Above left: Dropping down into the Biedouw Valley on the way to Wupperthal*

*Above right: Small settlement on top of the Kouberg between Wupperthal and Heuningvlei*

when Leipoldt saw the valley from the top of Kouberg, he apparently exclaimed that the name should be Wupperthal, in memory of the German valley housing the head office of the Rhenish Missionary Society. Despite the village retaining this name, the valley however is still known by its Khoi name of Tra-Tra, meaning 'bushy river'.

If the Strassberger family managed to commercialise and place the humble velskoen on the market, it was Wupperthal that can claim to be its birthplace. Leipoldt,

*Above: Original farmhouse, now the tearoom and information centre, Wupperthal*

one of the two missionaries who started Wupperthal, was the more practical craftsman and made a point of teaching his parishioners the crafts of millinery, shoe making, tanning, joinery and thatching. The shoe factory is still operational and their expertise in thatching is reflected in the tidy white thatched-roof houses lining the streets of the small village, housing 400 families. Other attractions include a rooibos tea factory, craft store and the very popular 4X4 trails into the Cederberg Wilderness Reserve through the impressive scenery in Kouberg and smaller villages like Heuningvlei.

I was keen to find out why the Rhenish missionaries chose this remote spot for a mission station, and I use the opportunity to find an answer at the information centre next door to the tearoom. While the two missionaries were exploring possible sites, the original farm Rietmond or reed mouth in Afrikaans, came up for sale and as there were already a few Khoikhoi families living on the farm, the Society purchased it. The thatched roof tearoom is actually the original farmhouse of Rietmond and the first building used by the missionaries.

On our way back we rejoin the N7 to the west of Clanwilliam. Although we will be leaving the fascinating Cederberg mountains, there is consolation in the fact that we will be staying with the Olifants River for the next part of the tour. The road takes us past the Clanwilliam and Bulshoek dams into the heart of the wine region of the Olifants River.

# 2. Matzikama

**West Coast Regional Tourism Organisation**
PO Box 242, Moorreesburg 7310
Tel: +27 (0)22 433 2380
Email: tourism@capewestcoast.org
Website: www.capewestcoast.org

**Matzikama Tourist Association**
Museum Building, Vanrhynsdorp 8170
Tel: +27 (0)27 219 1552
Email: vanrhynsdorp@matzikamamun.co.za
Website: www.tourismvanrhynsdorp.co.za

**Matzikama Tourist Association**
37 Church Street, PO Box 98
Vredendal 8160
Tel: +27 (0)27 201 3376
Email: tourism@matzikamamun.co.za
Website: www.tourismmatzikama.co.za

# 2. Matzikama

Just when you think that you have left the Olifants River behind, the next valley opens up, but this time the orange groves have been replaced by vineyards and tunnel farms. We have entered the irrigation section of the river and its first settlement, Trawal. Between the road and the river you can trace the irrigation canal until the road and a branch of the canal cross the Olifants River and the road climbs out of the valley.

Now even the mountains change. To our right we no longer have the ragged Cederberg range but the flat sandstone Matzikamma mountains, meaning water pools in Khoi. To talk about mountains is actually misleading because this is the one stretch along the western escarpment where the top of the mountains as seen from the river basin, is actually the floor of the Karoo high veld plateau. Three members in the range, Gifberg, Koebee and Maskam, are protruding into the Olifants River basin like sentinels, and especially Maskam is a well-known landmark in the area. Even these three mountains are flat on top and home to rooibos farmers.

There is one anomaly that took some effort to explain, namely why the mountain range is called Matzikamma and the district the Matzikama. The dispute is over the original Khoi spelling of the word 'kamma' and has not yet been resolved.

To our left is the river with its green belt of vineyards, a leading wine region of South Africa, made possible by irrigation. This irrigation system also resulted in the development of a group of towns, each with its unique charm to entice visitors. Anyone considering a break in this valley should allow the ambience of these places to dictate their choice of accommodation, as the choice can be difficult.

**Klawer**, named after the wild clover found nearby, is conveniently situated next to the N7 and on top of the river bank, overlooking the Olifants River. From here you have a panoramic view of the valley with its vineyards and tunnel farms,

**Vredendal** is the main town in the valley and is your best choice if you want good business, accommodation and shopping facilities,

**Lutzville** on the other hand is a low lying town in the valley surrounded by vineyards,

**Vanrhynsdorp** is also next to the N7 and should be the choice if you prefer free open space and the remarkable succulents of the Knersvlakte,

**Trawal, Spruitdrift** and **Koekenaap** are wine and tunnel farming communities in between, possibly with a small shop but very little else. Holiday accommodation here is likely to be on the farms.

*Above left: Irrigation canal and vineyards in the Olifants River basin*

*Above right: Maskam, seen from the Vredendal golf course*

# Valley Settlements

The fascinating history of the valley can be traced in phases of conflict, settlement, development, the gift of irrigation, and finally recognition.

## Conflict

After the initial wars between the Dutch and the Khoikhoi during the 17th century, tribes like the Grigriquas, found it safer and more convenient to settle on the plains in the Olifants river basin, but this did not necessarily mean peace and tranquillity. The Dutch explorers used Heerenlogement, the Dutch word for gentlemen's lodgings near Graafwater, and Fleermuijsklip or bat's rock, near Lutzville as stop-over caves during their early expeditions and the first migrant farmers soon discovered the area. Bartering and mutual cattle theft became rife, as proved by names still used today. The farm Bakkely Plaatz was supposedly named after a scrabble in 1668 when the local tribe tried to steal back the cattle they sold to the explorers. Similarly the farm Vreedensdal, later to become Vredendal, was apparently named after a peace treaty brokered by Simon van der Stel in 1685, either between two feuding Khoikhoi tribes, or between the Khoikhoi and the Dutch farmers according to another interpretation of the historical papers. The period of conflict continued into the early part of the 18th century, by which time the government negotiated and bought land from the Grigriquas to lease to white farmers.

## Settlement

The explorers were followed by the migrating farmers who settled in the valley, illegally in the beginning, and from around the mid 18th century with official grazing rights. The first two quitrent farms receiving grazing rights south of the Olifants River in 1732, belonged to Pieter van Zyl near the current Spruitdrift and Jacob Cloete at Heerenlogement. Today the surnames Van Zyl and Cloete are still numerous in the area. For that matter, Johanna's husband, Alk van Zyl, was a wine farmer near Spruitdrift, as were the husbands of her best friends, Engela van Zyl, whose son still has a wine farm near Lutzville, and Ena and Nici van Zyl who used to own the wine farm next to Johanna's and have now retired to Klawer. Farming during the 18th and 19th centuries was, however, predominantly livestock with limited agriculture and times were hard in this dry merciless land.

## Development

Even though the British, after colonisation in 1806, were really more interested in the southern and eastern parts of South Africa than the north-western coast, they encouraged the Missionary Societies to work with the indigenous tribes as a means of stabilisation and development. The Olifants River basin also benefited. Rhenish, Moravian and London Missionary Societies moved in to set up mission stations at Fleermuijsklip in 1817, and later at Wupperthal in 1830 and Ebenhaezer in 1831.

The missionaries not only tended their own flock, but offered the only formal schooling around. Most of the migrating farmers and settlers educated their children at home with the assistance of the bible until affluent farmers at Troe-Troe, Vanrhynsdorp in 1865, and Spruitdrift in 1888, could afford to set up private schools. Travelling teachers were used in these private schools with varying degrees of success, and it was only in 1904 that a government school opened for the lower Olifants River region at Spruitdrift.

The school had two holidays per year, saaityd or sowing time and oestyd or harvesting time, to enable the children to help on the farms. In the meantime the children from across the river could only reach the school by rowing boat, a treacherous journey when the river was in

*Above left: A view of the Clanwilliam Dam at the foot of the Cederberg mountains*

*Above right: The dam wall and sluice gates of the Clanwilliam Dam*

flood! This period however, knew some remarkable people. Wessel Ebersohn, for instance, was the first teacher at the Spruitdrift school, and also:

commissioner of oaths,

dentist (tooth extraction only!),

first aider,

helper with catechism classes, choir and prayer meetings,

member of the water board during the development of the irrigation scheme,

a founder member of the Nationalist political party,

member of various organisations, and

the proud owner of the first telephone in the community.

Truly a busy person and pillar of the local community! Vanrhynsdorp was the major town and when the Clanwilliam district was subdivided in 1892, Vanrhynsdorp became the seat of the district council for the lower Olifants River and Knersvlakte. Spruitdrift at this stage had a school and a post office and played a significant role in the community.

## Olifants River Irrigation Scheme

Farming still consisted mainly of livestock and limited arable farming. During the 1890s, however, a successful irrigation canal was constructed alongside the Gariep near Kakamas and this led to the idea that a similar scheme could work for the Olifants River as well.

In 1911 the area was proclaimed as the Olifants River Irrigation District and work commenced on the Bulshoek dam, near Trawal, and the canals in 1913. In 1924 the first canals became operational. The initial idea was to build the Bulshoek dam between Clanwilliam and Trawal to divert water from the river through sluice gates into the canals to feed the neighbouring farms. The dam was constructed according to a patent of Glenfield and Kennedy Ltd. from Kilmarnock with 16 sluice gates, each having three openings to let water out to the left. The single canal split south of Klawer. The southern branch of the canal initially serviced farms to Lutzville, but was extended to Ebenhaezer in 1978. The second branch of the canal crossed the river in a pipe to the northern side for the farms from Klawer to Koekenaap. As this canal had to service higher lying farms, eleven siphons and tunnels were constructed to raise the level of the water sufficiently.

The initial uptake of the water by the farmers was slow due to the price they had to pay, but Johan Lutz, the local engineering superintendent, persevered in marketing the idea and by 1981 the scheme boasted a complex of 261 km of main and 60 km of branch canals. Over 900 farmers were making use of the water to irrigate over a total of 10,500 ha of farmland.

As early as 1927 it became obvious that the Bulshoek dam was too small to meet the need of the farmers during the drier seasons, while wide-spread flooding was still a problem in winter. A second dam was proposed to collect enough water and to regulate floods, and the Clanwilliam Dam was constructed between 1932 and 1935. Although the construction of the Clanwilliam dam did not put a stop to all flooding, it became possible to regulate the water release from the dam and to manage the flood damage. Flooding during the winter months was actually found to be good for the crops because of the nutrients in the silt deposited by the water. Lutz was eventually honoured for his role in both the irrigation scheme projects by changing the name of Fleermuijsklip to Lutzville.

The system of water rights became so important that farms have been bought or sold for their water rights rather than for the land. Each farmer is entitled to a certain number of water hours per week when he can divert the water from the canal into his collection dam. He can choose to use his water hours in bursts or continuously for a weaker stream of water. In the past furrowing was the preferred method to water the crops, but nowadays nearly all farms use sprinkler and drip systems for economy and better results.

## Recognition

Although an early reference to wine making in the Olifants River Valley can be traced to the inventory submitted by Barend Lubbe on the farm Brakkefontein in 1775, the irrigation scheme allowed farmers to expand and venture further

away from the river. Places like Klawer, Vredendal, Lutzville, Koekenaap, Trawal and Spruitdrift thrived on the success of irrigation, and vineyards and vegetables became the staple crops. The railway line which was built from Cape Town to Klawer in 1910 furthermore brought the Cape market within reach for produce from the valley and individual cellars.

The Koöperatiewe Wijnbouwers Vereniging van Zuid Afrika Beperk, (KWV) was formed at Stellenbosch in 1918, to help with the regulation of the wine price which collapsed because of overproduction and the loss of the overseas market. Wine farmers from all over the Cape, including the Olifants River Valley, joined the KWV Co-operative society and started producing grapes on a quota system, mostly for distillation of the KWV brandy and some wines, for export. Only during the 1980s when the own label estate wines regained popularity, and in 1992 when the KWV was stripped of its governing powers, did the local cellars in the Valley re-emerged. Today this region is a major player in the local as well as the global wine markets and a visit to the cellars on the Olifants River Valley wine route is becoming a must for tourists.

## Olifants River wine route

The Olifants River wine route boasts eight top class cellars in addition to the number of emerging own label farmers. You can contact the local Information

Centres personally or on the internet to get the latest information on available cellars as the wine industry is vibrant and growing in the valley.

## Citrusdal

The Citrusdal Co-operative Wine Cellar specialises in wines from a variety of climatic regions, ranging from dry-land conditions near the coast to the higher rainfall areas in the Cederberg range and Piketberg.

## Cederberg

Dwarsrivier, a cellar specialising in high altitude vineyards, is a private farm 47 km on the Algeria road between Citrusdal and Clanwilliam.

## Trawal

The first cellar whose members benefit from the irrigation canal water downstream from the Bulshoek dam. They specialise in enjoyable drinking wines. The tasting cellar is alongside the N7 between Clanwilliam and Klawer.

## Klawer

A cellar committed to top quality and award winning wines. The cellar is off the N7 just before reaching Klawer.

## Spruitdrift

Part of Westcorp International Cellars, it specialises in red wines. The tasting cellar is situated at the Westcorp Cellar.

## Stoumann's

A private cellar aimed at producing top quality wines in small quantities for local and export markets. The tasting cellar is between Klawer and Vredendal shortly before reaching Vredendal.

## Westcorp International Cellars

Westcorp International Cellars Vredendal, is not only the largest cellar in South Africa, but in the southern hemisphere. Its innovative management team managed to produce and blend award winning wines for local and overseas tastes, substantiated by the fact that around 15 percent of all wines imported by the United Kingdom, comes from this cellar.

Westcorp International Cellars presses more grapes in one season than the whole of the New Zealand industry together. Wine is marketed under various labels, one of which is the popular Gôiya label which is San for first wine and is a blend of Chardonnay and Sauvignon Blanc. They also produce the Namaqua boxed wines which are very popular in the United Kingdom and Europe. The cellar is between Vredendal and Vanrhynsdorp, not far from the Vredendal golf course.

## Lutzville

Lutzville claims to have the most westerly cellar in South Africa, processing grapes exposed to the cooling climate from the Atlantic ocean. The tasting cellar is in Lutzville, right next to the golf club.

*Above: Vergenoeg Catholic Church at Vredendal*

## Private Cellars

Between Vredendal and Klawer private cellars have been and still are emerging at an amazing pace. It is important to check with the Information centres on the latest lists to ensure that you do not miss out on some of the outstanding wines of the region.

\*      \*      \*      \*

# Vredendal

Vredendal benefited most from the irrigation boom. Although it only received official town status in 1944 and municipal status in 1963, it became the seat of the Matzikama Municipality during the local government restructure in 2000, responsible for Vredendal, Vanrhynsdorp, Lutzville, Papendorp, Ebenhaezer, Klawer, Strandfontein and Doring Bay. As the leading business town of the area it offers modern shopping facilities, banks, internet cafes and all the amenities of a thriving town. We will be staying with Johanna, the final member of our group, in Vredendal. This will give us an opportunity to explore the Matzikama region and have a short holiday at the seaside before we start the tour along the north-western escarpment of the Cape.

What are the attractions in Vredendal once you have exhausted its modern business, banks and shopping facilities? We visit the well-equipped and helpful Information Centre next to the library to get the latest maps and information and plan the rest of our stay in Vredendal.

The Vergenoeg Catholic Church and school on the outskirts of Vredendal is our first stop. The mission dates back to 1935 when Father Archambaud bought the farm, named Vergenoeg or far enough by its owners, to start a church and school. The current church building was inaugurated in 1958 by Bishop Esser. In addition to the work of the nuns at the station, a major attraction of the church is its architecture. Theo Peeters, the architect,

## Vredendal
Full modern business facilities
Hotels, full range of accommodation
Restaurants

**Attractions:**
Historical buildings
Wine Cellars
Rittelfees (jive festival)
Hiking trails
Flowers in spring

*Above left: Melkboomsdrift, an early farmhouse near Lutzville, now a guesthouse*

*Above right: Grapes, ready for harvesting*

wanted the church to be a landmark to the glory of God. In order to achieve this he designed the church in the Roman style, using the Christian holy numbers of 3 and 7 throughout the building - three towers, seven arches, steps in multiples of three or seven, and the use of colours to indicate various messages. He succeeded admirably in his mission.

Dave and Paul are more interested in a game of golf on the grass course of the Vredendal Golf Club. This is followed by visits to the next door Westcorp International Cellars, the biggest in the southern hemisphere, and other private cellars like Stoumann's. Janey and I on the other hand are happy to go with Johanna on a drive past the old farmhouse of the original Vreedensdal farm next to the river (now a private residence), and then on for a cup of tea at the local nursery. The nursery is on the road to Klawer and is not only popular for its wide selection of all types of garden plants, including fully grown trees, but also has a popular tearoom in the garden.

Unfortunately we are missing out on the Rittelfees and other local festivals. The Rittelfees, Afrikaans for jive festival, could be described as the Glastonbury of the western coast and attracts musical groups and visitors from all over the country during the four day musical extravaganza on the sports grounds of Vredendal in October.

## *Lutzville*

The visit to Lutzville and Koekenaap takes us through the farm communities in the valley, but with some added surprises like Vlermuisklip, the Sishen railway bridge and the Kliphuis.

Lutzville was formerly known as Fleermuijsklip, named after the large rock cave presumably inhabited by bats, where early explorers used to camp during the 17th century. The name was changed to honour Johan Lutz for his contributions towards the irrigation scheme. Today

31

# 2. MATZIKAMA

*Above left: Sishen/Saldanha bridge over the Olifants River near Lutzville*

*Above right: Working roses planted as borders alongside the vineyards*

---

the rock is known as the Vlermuisklip, Afrikaans for bat's rock, and is a national monument. You can view the rock paintings and marks against the rock walls where the elephants used to rub themselves.

On our way to the Sishen railway bridge, just before Lutzville, we pass Melkboomsdrift, one of the oldest farmhouses in the region, built in 1825 and now a popular guesthouse and a national monument. The temptation is too great and we stop for tea and scones before continuing. From the house you have an

excellent view of the vineyards in the Olifants River valley, a great introduction to the sites we planned for the day.

The Sishen-Saldanha bridge, our next stop, has nothing to do with Lutzville, except that it towers over the valley near the town. Sishen is a mining town to the north-west of Upington, where in middle of the 20th century the richest find of iron ore in South Africa was discovered. A major problem for the mining company was the remoteness of the site, and how to find a way to economically transport the ore to a port. As there is no deep water harbour along the western coast of South Africa, the nearest suitable destination happened to be Saldanha Bay on the south-west Cape coast, 860 km away. Most of the route would cross the flat Karoo and Sandveld plains, and a railway line was built from Sishen all the way to Saldanha during the 1970s with the sole purpose of transporting iron ore to the coast.

One of the more difficult parts was to decide how to cross the Olifants River

## Lutzville
Basic business facilities
Hotel, full range of accommodation

**Attractions:**
Historical sites
Sishen-Saldanha bridge
Wine Cellars
Hiking

valley en route. The trains had to be long to be economical and it was essential to eliminate any unnecessary gradients along the way, as it would be virtually impossible for the engines to get the trains moving again on even a slight incline. A bridge over the valley was the answer. The French company Spie Batignols completed the bridge in 1976, one of the largest of its kind in the world. The bridge is 1,035 m in length, consists of 23 sections of 45 m each, resting on pillars, the highest of which measure 52.5 m. The deck of the bridge eventually weighed 141,000 tons and each section had to be slid into position with the help of massive hydraulic jacks over teflon sheets. Since its completion the kilometre long trains have become an everyday sight.

Lutzville is in the valley of the Olifants River and the drive through the town to the farm of Engela's son is scenic. On both sides of the road are the vineyards, adorned by rows of flowering rose bushes next to the road. It was during a holiday in Australia that I learnt the secret of the rose bushes. I always admired the aesthetic taste of the farmers until a wine farmer told us that roses are susceptible to the same type of pests and diseases as vines, but display earlier symptoms of the disease. The roses are therefore working plants and not cultivated for decorative purposes! Never mind, the flowers still add to the beauty of the scenery.

Lutzville also has a popular grass golf course, but the popularity has a twist, as the 18th hole is right next to the tasting rooms of the Lutzville Wine Cellar. No wonder that golf and wine tasting are often combined as popular attractions in Lutzville.

Engela invited us to their farm outside Lutzville to observe how raisins are dried and to watch a grape harvester in action. It is easy to identify the export vines as the whole vineyard is covered by mesh against damage, especially from birds. The bunches are still picked by hand, carefully graded and checked for quality before being folded in tissue

*Above left:  Harvesting grapes for the cellars with a harvester*

*Above right:  Collection dam on a farm to collect the water from the canal*

*Above: Tomatoes picked for pulping by the local Co-operative*

**Koekenaap**
Basic business facilities
Guest houses, self catering
Traditional cuisine restaurant

**Attractions:**
Historical sites
Vineyards

and packed in the boxes. The cellars on the other hand nowadays prefer machine harvested grapes for wine as there will be no stalks for them to remove. These vines are planted and trained in narrow straight rows to a height of around two metres. The harvester, a beast of a machine, then straddles a row and literally shakes and strips the grapes off the stalks. At the end of two rows, the grapes are tipped into a truck for later delivery to the cellar. Dave even managed to hitch a ride on the machine for one round trip.

The preparation of raisins is again a different process. Hanepoot, a sweet white grape, is often the preferred choice for raisins. Bunches are either hung on racks covered with mesh, or the grapes are spread on large cement floors to dry in the sun. This is becoming a scarce sight in the Olifants River valley as it is not as economical as the wine or export grapes. We will later find that raisins are more a product from Kakamas than Vredendal.

Although the Olifants River irrigation region is primarily known for its wines, many farmers are growing vegetables as an alternative, or as supporting crops and tunnel farming has become quite popular. As we leave the farm to go back to Vredendal, we can see harvesting in progress on a tomato farm. Tomatoes are hand picked into crates for delivery to the local Co-operative where they are pulped and transported to the Cape for further processing into soups and sauces.

# Koekenaap

Koekenaap, more a collection of farms than a village, is on the opposite side of the river from Lutzville. It was not easy to trace the origin of the name Koekenaap and the ones included here are only two of a variety of explanations. One tongue-in-cheek explanation is that two German missionaries apparently stopped at the top of the river bank near Koekenaap where the one exclaimed 'guck hinab', look down there, at the beauty of the scenery below, and the derivation of this exclamation stuck as its name! Another possibility is that the Khoi

## Klawer

Basic business facilities
Hotel, full range of accommodation

**Attractions:**
Historical sites
Wine Cellars
Hikes and river sport
Flowers in spring

*Above: Klawer church steeple seen from the palm trees in the park*

translation could mean 'the river where the meat was cut', but why the meat was cut, is not known. Maybe the name has some link with the Kliphuis eatery along the river bank which specialises in local cuisine. This is quite a popular venue for interesting meals served underneath a rocky overhang, but you may have to book in advance as they only cater for 10 or more guests at time!

## *Klawer*

The road between Vredendal and Klawer, for our next visit, is one of my favourites as it follows the river and the vineyards all the way. Sometimes you can only see a strip of green, gradually expanding to show the valley in its full glory, and then again you are faced with the contrast of the vineyards offset against the bare hills away from the river. Just before Klawer we reach the bridge over the river, after which the road climbs to the top of the hill where it crosses the railway line and station to our left. Klawer can trace

its origins to this railway line. During the construction of the line between 1910 and 1915, Klawer, as the proposed terminus, housed the railway workers and a town developed around the camp. When the N7 was constructed during the latter half of the 20th century, many of the road construction workers were also stationed here. Today Klawer is a neat town, proud of its palm tree lanes and parks.

Klawer offers activities for at least three kinds of visitors. The action seeker can join in river rafting on the Doring River which joins the Olifants River nearby, and the connoisseur can visit the Klawer Cellars off the N7. Historians can visit the sites of the Anglo Boer War skirmishes between troops of General Smuts and the British in 1902 on the nearby farm Windhoek, on appointment with the farmer. It was on this farm where Lemuel (Lambert) Colyn was found hiding in the farm house chimney and later executed as a traitor in February 1902.

We are however happy with the social nature of our visit for today. Ena and Nici

*Above left: Vanrhynsdorp Succulent Nursery*
*Left: Quiver trees*
*Above: Young halfmens (half human) trees*

van Zyl retired to Klawer and invited us to Nici's birthday celebration. Like most South African men Nici's speciality is outside cooking, usually a braai. The menu tonight is grilled fish, Portuguese style, well salted and then grilled over the coals, accompanied by the usual selection of salads, bread and cake to follow. There is one more dish which I have not had for years and can be described as the west coast haggis. It is locally referred to as puff adder, as it resembles a snake when cooked. The fatty intestine of a sheep is properly cleaned inside and outside, and left with the fat inside. It is tied at the one end, stuffed with strips of well flavoured fillet steak or liver, and grilled over the coals like sausage, quite a delicacy. The evening is a great success with all their family and friends around and we feel honoured to have been included in the group.

## Vanrhynsdorp and the Knersvlakte

Vanrhynsdorp, our next destination, developed on the farm Troe-Troe which received grazing rights in 1751. The name was changed to Vanrhynsdorp in 1880 after PB van Rhijn, the owner of

## Vanrhynsdorp

All business facilities
Hotel, full range of accommodation
Restaurants

**Attractions:**
Historical buildings and museums
Historical sites
Succulent nursery and trails
Waterfall and flowers in spring

the farm and benefactor to the village. Like Clanwilliam, Vanrhynsdorp retained its Victorian atmosphere. The visit to Vanrhynsdorp takes us away from the river to introduce us to the Knersvlakte, unique in all respects.

The Knersvlakte stretches for approximately 450,000 ha to the north and east of Vanrhynsdorp, and is typified by low rolling hills with patches of small white quartz pebbles and very saline soil. The name Knersvlakte or crunchy plain, apparently refers to the sound when walking or driving over these pebbles.

For the uninformed eye the scenery may seem bleak and boring to the point of being repulsive. This particular spot, however, encompasses one of the most remarkable exhibits of cryptic behaviour of plants anywhere in the world. The succulents not only learnt to adapt to the environment for survival, but are actually mimicking their stony surroundings to prevent them from being recognised as a nutritious meal by the animals. There are between 600 and 800 species of succulents, more than 140 of which are endemic to the area.

We spend a very interesting and informative afternoon at the Kokerboom Nursery in Vanrhynsdorp admiring their vast collection of succulents from the western coast region as well as other parts of South Africa. Not only is it fascinating to see how the succulents have adapted to survive in harsh climates but we will be seeing quite a few of them in their natural surroundings on the tour and might as well do some hands-on research here. Plants are ranging from the tall kokerboom, or quiver tree (Aloe dichotoma) and halfmens (Pachypidium namaquanum) which grow on the rocky outcrops and mountains further north, to the small succulents which you have to search for amongst the pebbles and rocks. Approximately 25 km north of Vanrhynsdorp, the nursery offers a three kilometre succulent hiking trail on their farm where these plants occur in their natural surroundings, a must if you are interested in succulents and other Karoo plants.

Two of the locally common, but at the same time more unusual succulents are the stone flower and the partridge aloe. The silver stone flower (argyroderma delaetii) or more aptly known as bababoudjies, Afrikaans for baby bottoms, is 5 cm high and only consists of two globular smooth leaves moulded together to give the impression of a single unit. During the dry summer months the leaves shrink, thus allowing the plant to hide unseen amongst the quartz pebbles. Between April and June a daisy like flower appears between the leaves, much bigger than the plant itself and in bright colours from yellow to purple. The partridge aloe (Aloe variegate), better known as kanniedood, Afrikaans for cannot die, or choje in San, is a small aloe with stacked and distinctly speckled leaves, growing on dry stony flats along the west of South Africa. It has relatively large pink or red candle shaped flowers in spring and was chosen as the emblem of the Griquas, as we will find out later. Both can be found in abundance on the Knersvlakte together with the other interesting succulents.

During April, this area becomes a real floral showcase and that is the time to venture on to the plains or to visit the ongoing succulent shows at the Kokerboom Nursery. Similarly, August and September are the best months to drive to Urionskraal Valley between the Maskam and Koebee mountains. Here you can visit the waterfall behind Maskam and observe the spring flowers. The name Gifberg or poisonous mountain, the third mountain in the Matzikamma range, has an interesting origin. It apparently refers to the poisonous seeds of the Hyaenanche globosa plant used by the San to cover the tips their arrows for hunting.

We stop at the information centre in Vanrhynsdorp for a very interesting discussion with the manager at the centre. We enquire about the impact of the Anglo Boer War on the town and he directs us to the house where General Smuts stayed

*Above left: Typical vegetation and quartzite pebbles of the Knersvlakte*

*Above right: Partridge aloe (kanniedood), the emblem of the Griquas*

*Right: Stoneflower succulents (bababoudjies) on the Knersvlakte*

*Above: One of the matjieshuise (reed huts) on the Ratelgat development village*

*Right: The Griqua monument at Ratelgat and the Knersvlakte in the background*

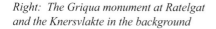

during the short periods when the Boer forces occupied Vanrhynsdorp in 1901, and the nearby war graves. The Van Rhijn museum dating back to 1897 covers the history of the area and, fortunately, we arranged a visit to the Latsky museum as well. This museum is usually only open during the flower season and contains a private collection of more than 200 valve radios dating back to the 1920s, causing many exclamations of 'do you remember' from members of the group.

The next morning we collect Valerie Mentoor at the Vredendal information centre. She is a local tour guide and promised to take us on an informal tour to one of the new Biosphere Reserve projects, still under development in the Knersvlakte - a visit to Ratelgat.

## Ratelgat

In the year 1916, Andrew Abraham Stockenström (AAS) le Fleur, the paramount chief of one of the Griqua tribes, arrived at the farm Ratelgat.

The story of Ratelgat starts with his story, also known as the story of 'Die Kneg van God', or just simply Die Kneg (the Servant of God). Chief le Fleur was born in 1867 in Hirschell in the Orange Free State and became paramount chief to the le Fleur branch of the Griquas when he married Rachel Susanna Kok, the daughter of Adam Kok III. His major contribution to the Griqua nation was however much more than being a leader. At a relatively early age he became known as a soothsayer and following an inner call, he moved to Ratelgat in 1915 from where his predictions and moral lessons as Die Kneg were recorded in his letters to members of his tribe, and are still widely used. Although he left Ratelgat in 1933 and was buried at Robberg, near Plettenberg Bay, after his death in 1941, his predictions and guidance still play a major role in the lives of his followers.

Some of his predictions include:

The exact date and time he would be released from prison, the first time he was imprisoned in the beginning of the 20th century (it happened as he predicted).

That a railway line will pass close to Ratelgat (the current Sishen-Saldanha line).

That the Griqua nation will be reunited, especially on the farm Ratelgat which they will obtain at no cost to themselves (granted to them in 1999).

He also believed in non-violence and the power of music, singing and prayer to defuse explosive situations and today the executive council of the le Fleur Griquas includes a board for music and culture to manage the choir and dance groups in the community.

Since the start of the Ratelgat and Luiperskop Griqua Development Centre in 1999, the farm Ratelgat has become a focal point for Griqua gatherings such as in June 2004 when approximately 3,000 followers of Chief Abraham le Fleur gathered around the monument on the farm for his funeral. They are also conducting regular religious gatherings on the farm to commemorate their national and religious days.

Developments are in progress to develop Ratelgat and adjacent Luiperskop into tourist and backpacker resorts without distracting from the use of the area for the Griqua celebrations. We are honoured to have been given a preview of the reed hut village still under construction and the monument, already well established. The village is especially interesting as the huts are built by hand according to traditional methods, while containing modern shower and ablution facilities. A local kitchen and craft shop is also planned next to the road and a possible observatory near Luiperskop - all within the next two to three years.

\*     \*     \*     \*

And now we really need that holiday at Strandfontein. A holiday within a holiday may sound daft, but then Strandfontein is different and has always been associated with holidays.

# 3. Seaside Holidays

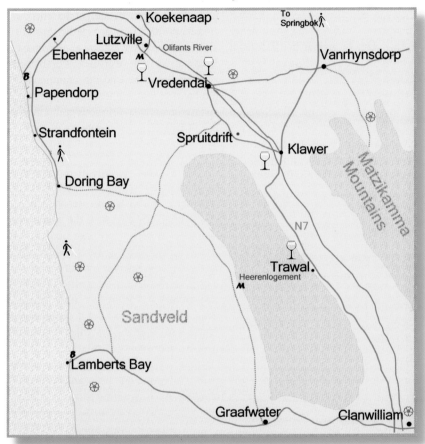

**West Coast Regional Tourism Organisation**
PO Box 242, Moorreesburg 7310
Tel: +27 (0)22 433 2380
Email: tourism@capewestcoast.org
Website: www.capewestcoast.org

**Matzikama Tourist Association**
37 Church Street, PO Box 98
Vredendal 8160
Tel: +27 (0)27 201 3376
Email: tourism@matzikamamun.co.za
Website: www.tourismmatzikama.co.za

**Lamberts Bay Tourism Bureau**
Church Street, PO Box 245
Lamberts Bay 8130
Tel: +27 (0)27 432 1000
Email: reslb@kingsley.co.za

**Clanwilliam Tourism Bureau**
Main Road, PO Box 5
Clanwilliam 8135
Tel: +27 (0)27 482 2024
Email: cederberg@lando.co.za
Website: www.clanwilliam.co.za

# 3. Seaside Holidays

## Diary of a farmer's wife
## December 1904

### Wednesday, early morning

It is still dark outside. I can hear Jan, my husband, boiling water in the kitchen for an early cup of coffee before going out to tend the sheep. Today will be a very busy day and I complete my mental checklist while stealing a few extra minutes in bed. Siena, my Griqua helper, and I must finish the baking, and then start packing all the provisions for our annual seaside holiday at Strandfontein. I have checked the list so often that I know it off by heart:

Iron pots for cooking, kettle and the grid for the braai,

Flour, yeast, maize meal, fat and seasoning for bread and porridge,

Dried beans and pulses for soups and stews,

Biltong, droë wors and bokkoms for snacks,

Beskuit, skuinskoek, koeksisters and dried fruit for the sweet tooth,

Potatoes, pumpkins, other long-life vegetables for meals, and anything else on the actual list.

The boys already left yesterday to find a good camping site, set up the matjieshuis, dig a hole for our fresh-water box near the fountain and to build a pen for the sheep, nanny goat and the few chickens that we are taking for meat, milk and eggs. The nearest, and only, farm shop is at Viswater, far enough to be discarded and we have to take along everything we might need. The excitement has really gripped everyone at home but there is still a lot to do.

### Thursday evening

I am bone tired but still too active to go to sleep. We left the farm near Vanrhynsdorp before sunrise and the journey in the mule wagon took all day along the sandy tracks. I spent most of the time on the wagon, to get a better view of the game, especially the springbok and steenbok, but we also saw tortoises and a porcupine. Two incidents helped to alleviate the boredom of the journey. The first came when a yellow cobra slithered across the road and the mules nearly took flight, and the second was when we got stuck in the sand not far from Strandfontein. We all had to help to dislodge the wagon.

Luckily our sons had a roaring fire going on arrival and after quickly sorting out the sleeping arrangements, we could sit down to our first braai at the seaside. Some of the family and friends came around to greet us, but to be honest we were all too tired to participate much and will make up for it tomorrow.

### Sunday afternoon

Today is Sunday, and writing the diary is one of the few activities allowed on the Holy Day. The Reverend Basson from Vredendal delivered the morning sermon on the beach and I must admit it was easy to let your mind wander during his two hour sermon.

The last few days absolutely flew by. After the daily breakfast of porridge, bread and meat, it was time to visit my family and friends, and to catch up on the latest local gossip and news of who married whom, new additions to the families and other news. The young ones formed a nice crowd and spent most of the time playing games on the beach while the men fished and hunted for the pot, or competed in various contests. Some even ventured into the cold water for a splash, the women near the camp and the men further along the beach.

The main meal usually takes place late afternoon. The stew would have been simmering in the black iron pot since lunch time on the days that we do not have a braai. Before bedtime I will prepare the yeast and dough for tomorrow's bread to be baked in an outside oven built by the men, or as potbrood in a flat bottom iron pot. Luckily the girls help with the dishes to give me and Siena some time off. Except for the young ones with permission to stay up a bit later, bedtime is early.

## Wednesday morning

I can't believe that we will be going back tomorrow. The New Year's Eve dance lived up to its usual fun and expectation. It was held in the barn of the farm house, and the Nel brothers played the concertina, banjo and guitar. Siena and I helped at the cake and ginger beer table, which became ever more popular with the youngsters as the evening progressed. After the communal braai which the men handled, we even managed to join the youngsters for a few dances on the floor. I am glad they are enjoying it. It can be a very lonely life when you are young on a farm. Today, however will be spent on packing and tomorrow morning after the final dismantling of the matjieshuis, it will be the long trek back to the farm and another year of drought and hardships.

\*     \*     \*     \*

## Diary of our holiday January 2004

Even during the planning stage of the tour, we decided on a week of leisure to mentally prepare ourselves for the rest of the trip. I cannot think of a more suitable location than Strandfontein, 45 km from Vredendal, for this holiday.

## Wednesday afternoon

Johanna explained where I must pick up the keys to the log cabin we have rented for the week, while Dave, our self-appointed chef is stocking up. As the café at Strandfontein only stocks the absolute basics, and we are expecting Johanna and

*Above left: The palm lane entrance to Strandfontein with the hall in the background*
*Above right: Strandfontein village around the fresh water spring on the beach (dark spot)*
*Below left: Looking down at the Hell or Fryer's Cove at Strandfontein*
*Below right: Fishing from the rocks in Fryer's Cove*

her children from the Cape to join us over the weekend, Dave is ensuring that our fridge and freezer in Strandfontein will be crammed with food, enough to feed an army. The essentials include:

Boerewors, chops, steaks and the delicious smoked pork rib for the braai (frozen if not for consumption in the next couple of days),

Karringmelk beskuit, koeksisters, and some cream cakes from the local delicatessen for tea-time snacks,

Fruit in season, including pawpaws, melons, figs, grapes and mangoes.

Dried fruit strips and sliced biltong, ready vacuum packed for snacks,

The usual fresh vegetables and salad,

Bread from the local bakeries, including the delicious nutty bread you can buy,

Wine, beer, cans of cool drink and the essential gin and tonic for the ladies at sundown.

Anything else that we may need like fresh milk, can be bought at the local shop, or a drive to Doring Bay or Vredendal will provide an easy option.

The provisions do not include any fish as Dave and Johan promised fresh fish from the sea, but ever hopeful that the women of today can still remember some of the domestic crafts of yesterday, Dave also includes the necessary ingredients for scones and muffins. Janey eventually relented and treated us to home made scones and muffins before the end of the week!

## Strandfontein

Strandfontein, named after the fresh water fountain literally on the beach, is still only a holiday resort. When a crayfish factory was erected in Doring Bay in 1926, the district council at Vanrhynsdorp decided that Strandfontein would not be able to entice permanent residents without any opportunities of employment, so they decided to develop Doring Bay as a town and leave Strandfontein as a resort. Strandfontein of today is however a holiday resort with an extremely well developed and managed infrastructure, supporting the full range from picnic facilities and camping, to luxury holiday homes and a few guest houses. During Christmas and Easter holidays the place is teeming with holiday makers as it has been for the past 150 years, but any other time you can have the town to yourself and the slowly growing number of retired people who now live there permanently. There is only one basic shop in the town, but this adds to its romance and charm.

### Strandfontein
Limited business facilities
Guesthouses, self catering, camping

### Attractions
Fishing
swimming and beach activities
Hiking
Flowers in spring

## Thursday evening

The trip to Strandfontein takes just over half an hour on a well maintained tarred road. Dave only had to swerve once to miss a tortoise with a death wish, trying to cross the road, but otherwise all went smoothly. You enter Strandfontein via a lane of palm trees leading from the main road to the information office. Here you can get details on accommodation, tide times for the fishermen, camping permits and general information.

The town drops quite steeply towards the beach and forms a horseshoe around the original fresh water spring, still visible on the beach. The centre part consists of a terraced, well laid out and equipped camp and caravan park with more public chalets, camping and picnic sites on the beach. The houses clearly mark the development stages over the years. Along the beach front you can see some of the prefabricated houses that were first erected during the 1960s and 1970s when plots could be leased for five years and the town slowly changed from a holiday

*Above left: Papendorp Eco Tourism Guest House next to the Olifants River Estuary*

*Above right: Boats waiting to be taken into the Olifants River Estuary for fishing*

camping site to the permanent structure of today. Higher up along the ridge are the more recent houses, built since the 1980s, some of which are palatial and a clear expression of their owners' wealth.

From the fountain a sandy beach stretches northwards all the way to the mouth of the Olifants River, but to the south it is a complete contrast. Rocky cliffs, ten metres high or more, form the coastline from the southern border of Strandfontein to immediately north of Doring Bay. The one significant gap in this rugged terrain is the ravine next to Strandfontein referred to as the Hell, or Fryer's Cove. The name Fryer's Cove refers to Richard Fryer, the son of Irish immigrants from Clanwilliam, who once owned the farm Hollebaksfontein on which Strandfontein developed. Calling the cove 'the Hell' conjures the picture of the sea at its worst, lashing out at the cliffs in stormy weather.

Our rented holiday home is a log cabin half way up the incline. The balcony overlooks the bay and most of the town, and we soon settle into our holiday roles and activities. Dave and Johan's aim is to catch as many fish as possible and they are sorting out their tackle and monitoring the tides. Paul, having spent his working life in the Merchant Navy and on research boats, is not interested in fishing, but willing to go along to improve his suntan, or else to read on the balcony while keeping an eye on the dolphins playing in the surf. Janey and I plan to explore the town, surrounding beaches and hills on foot, or just to relax with a book.

## Papendorp
Limited business facilities
Guesthouse

**Attractions:**
Fishing
Salt pans
RAMSAR Bird Sanctuary
Hiking

## Friday evening

In an earnest attempt to fill the pots with fresh seafood, Johan and Dave have tried to catch some fish from the cliffs and the rocks in Fryer's Cove, but only managed to reel in one small sand shark. Today, however the plan is to go back to the mouth of the Olifants River where in years gone by they were able to catch enough black tail and other fish for a feast at home. The road to the river mouth leads past Papendorp and into the recently proclaimed Olifants River Estuary.

## Papendorp

Papendorp has a chequered history indirectly linked to the Olifants River irrigation scheme. When in 1924, the irrigation canal was completed to Lutzville, the government purchased the farm Viswater (fish water) at the mouth of the Orange River and convinced the local inhabitants of the Fleermuijsklip mission station to be resettled to Viswater, then renamed Papendorp. The residents of Papendorp earn their living from fishing and the salt pans near the village. You can buy fresh fish directly from the fishermen even at Strandfontein.

The whole area around the river mouth, the Olifants River Estuary, has recently been recognised as a RAMSAR wet land site and an IBA (Important Bird Area). At the Ecotourism Guesthouse in Papendorp, visitors can stay to watch the sandpipers and other migratory waders frequenting this area. Over 180 species have already been recorded here to date.

Janey and I are however preparing to travel a bit further along the river to visit Ebenhaezer as well.

## Ebenhaezer

The first mission work at Ebenhaezer dates back to 1817 when the Rhenish missionaries were invited by the Griqua tribal chief, Kees Lewies. Baron von Wurmb who founded the mission station

*Above left: Dutch Reformed Mission Church at Ebenhaezer*

*Above right: Agricultural smallholdings at Ebenhaezer*

47

> **Ebenhaezer**
> Limited business facilities
> Some accommodation
>
> **Attractions:**
> Olifants River Estuary
> Mission Church
> Bird watching
> Hiking

coast due to over-fishing, but I am more pessimistic and would like to place some blame on the ever growing and continuous vacuuming of the sea-bed by the dredgers in search of diamonds. A permanent large dredger owned by the De Beers diamond company can be seen in the deeper water, while local dredgers are working the shallower waters as licensees. I hope their finds weigh up to the damage they cause to the sea-bed, however small it may be.

at Wupperthal, officially established a Rhenish station at Ebenhaezer in 1931 and this was taken over by the Dutch Reformed Mission Church after the Rhenish order decided to withdraw in 1889. The congregation includes Papendorp, but that is the end of the similarities between the two communities. When the irrigation canal was extended from Lutzville to Ebenhaezer in 1978, life at Ebenhaezer changed considerably. Today lucerne and other crops flourish on the small plots along the canal as a testament to what can be achieved with effort and help from the irrigation scheme. The village stretches along the river bank, and includes an impressive church building, thriving school, modern library, council buildings and a few shops.

I am afraid the fishing trip has again not been very successful. Johan is convinced that they have been using the wrong bait and should have tried to get hold of a suction pump to extract sand shrimp from the beach at the river mouth. Dave on the other hand is convinced that there are no more fish around the

## Sunday evening

Johanna arrived yesterday joined by her children and their families. She is staying with us but the others are occupying another family holiday home, except for the social meal times and braais which we all share. We have not seen them for more than a year and the chattering continued late into Saturday night.

## Tuesday

It is our last full day at Strandfontein and the day of the big hike to Doring Bay. We decide to delay our departure until at least four o'clock when the temperature will be cooler. Dave and Paul will be 'walking the car' so that we can have transport back to Strandfontein and also to include a quick visit to Fryer's Cove, the vineyard closest to the cold Atlantic ocean, which has just started to produce its own brand of wines.

As I expected, the seven kilometre walk is going very well. The track is clearly marked on top of the cliffs and is

*Above left: Hiking along the cliff tops from Strandfontein to Doring Bay*

*Above right: Cliffs along the coast near Strandfontein with a diamond dredger in the background*

relatively level. It is amazing how much more you notice and hear without other distractions around. Against a small hill at least a dozen ibis are feasting. It must be on something special, because when they notice us, they fly up, circle for a few minutes and land again at the same spot to resume the meal! All around us are bushes of summer yellow, white and purple vygies (Mesembryanthemum family) in full bloom and some other flowers which we do not know. This is what I love about the Sandveld along the coast. The sea mist provides enough moisture for the plants to have an evergreen appearance and at the slightest excuse to celebrate life in flower.

We are walking along the cliff edge which is on our right. The high ragged cliffs drop straight down to the sea, making for terrifying but impressive views. We pass at least two small memorials where a child and a young man died in accidental falls down the cliffs, but the beauty of the sun's reflection on the water against the stark rocks softens the scene. Further away from the shore we spot a few dolphins and the odd seal. During spring the southern right whales can also be observed off the coast.

## Doring Bay

As we approach Doring Bay, we can see the lighthouse from afar, and the coastline changes. The rocks give way to sandstone walls, which have been excavated for road building over the years and only left the scars as a reminder.

Our exciting find in this area are the heaps of mussel shells off the water's edge. These could be middens, regarded as proof of prehistoric habitation of the area by the San. It is humbling to come face to face with ancient history and the struggle for food while we are on our way to a lavish meal at the restaurant in Doring Bay.

*Above left: The Cabin seafood restaurant in Doring Bay*

*Above right: Doring Bay lighthouse, factory and pier*

The Cabin, dubbed 'The Titanic' by the locals because of the wreck in front, is well known for its excellent seafood. Janey and I have calamari steaks while the rest enjoy fish. Two incidents capture the spirit of the place. Firstly, it must be the first restaurant I have come across where the chef returns in person to recommend a different kind of fish, because it has been freshly caught today and therefore better value for money; and the second is the wine. I mentioned that Dave and Paul visited the Fryer's Cove estate. Lanzerac Cellars, near Stellenbosch, have just started to produce a Sauvignon Blanc wine from the grapes of Fryer's Cove and although supply is restricted to two exclusive hotels in Cape Town and Johannesburg, The Cabin managed to obtain a few bottles for its restaurant. We duly order and enjoy a bottle with our meal. The label on the bottle aptly tells the story of the vineyard.

'Wines forged of the earth, tempered by the sea.

This unique wine is made with grapes from the ward closest to the cold Atlantic Ocean on the west coast of South Africa, adjacent to the seaside resort of Strandfontein. Vines were planted amongst the beach vegetation 850 m from the sea and 20 m above sea level. This area was sought for its ideal cold weather climate, which imparts prominent flavour and character to the wine. The remarkable Fryer family, after whom the wine and nearby cove

## Doring Bay

Basic business facilities
Guest house, self catering
Seafood restaurant

**Attractions:**
Crayfish canning factory
Fishing, crayfishing
Hiking, flowers in spring

are named, established the first farm in this area and were also involved in the development of the local community.'

It is still light enough after the meal to take a few sunset photos of Doring Bay. During the week we popped in to Doring Bay for emergency purchases as it is the nearest working town to Strandfontein. The town boasts a guest house, well stocked shops, including a bait and fish shop, the crayfish canning factory for employment, and of course The Cabin restaurant to attract visitors and locals. Another interesting titbit is that the Catholic church at Doring Bay is apparently a smaller version of the church in Vredendal, also using the numbers three and seven throughout the architecture.

We spend the last evening on the balcony of our cabin, overlooking the lights of Strandfontein and their reflection in the black waters of the sea. It is so peaceful that we even forget how the early morning mist sometimes obscures

the view of the beach. As always it would have been nice if the time spent here could have been longer. Tomorrow we have one more coastal detour to make via Lamberts Bay and Heerenlogement on our way back to Vredendal.

## Wednesday evening

A coastal highway is currently under construction all the way from Cape Town along the coast to Vredendal. It has already been tarred up to Elands Bay and once complete, is likely to benefit the coastal towns all the way to Strandfontein. Unfortunately we cannot wait for that day and have to be satisfied with the drive along a somewhat corrugated dirt road from Doring Bay to Lamberts Bay.

# Lamberts Bay

Lamberts Bay is another fishing and crayfish canning town, already quite popular as a holiday resort. The town developed around the 1800s and was named after Admiral Robert Lambert who was the commander at the Cape from 1820 and who charted this coastline during the 1820s. In 1918 the Lamberts Bay Canning Company was established and became the lifeblood of the town.

We are having our lunch at a small restaurant near the harbour, next to the canning factory and order crayfish or rock lobster, also referred to as the red gold of Lamberts Bay due to the red colour that

---

### Lamberts Bay
All business facilities
Hotel, full range of accommodation
Seafood and traditional restaurants

**Attractions:**
Historical buildings and museums
Crayfish canning factory
Bird Island
Fishing, crayfishing, boating
Hiking, flowers in spring

---

the shells obtain after boiling. This spot is convenient for watching the fishing boats in the harbour and as the start of the short walk to Bird Island Nature Reserve. Bird Island is linked to the harbour by means of a breakwater and is home to thousands of Cape gannets, cormorants, terns and even a few penguins. The bird hide offers a close-up view of the birds without interference to them and we spend some time in the hide and viewing other displays on the island. It is estimated that the colony of birds deposits over 300 tons of guano on the island each year, creating quite a lucrative fertiliser business.

In 1901 an incident, jocularly referred to as 'the only naval action of the South African Boer War' occurred in the Bay when members of the Boer commando apparently fired at HMS Sybille and two other warships anchored in the harbour. Needless to say, there were no casualties. Shortly after this event, while all the officers were on shore leave, the crew took the ship into deeper water during a storm, only to have it wrecked on rocks

10 km south of Lamberts Bay near Steenbokfontein. The wreck is still visible at low tide and the propeller is on display in the garden of the Sandveld museum in Lamberts Bay. The Plaaskombuis (farm kitchen) restaurant at Steenbokfontein is a mine of information on this and other historical events, as well as being one of the traditional restaurants around the Bay.

On the way to Steenbokfontein we pass another restaurant, namely Muisbosskerm or mouse bush shelter, the first open air restaurant along the coast. Open on Sundays, it offers a seafood braai where you can literally gorge yourself, buffet style, with as much grilled seafood as you can handle. A third popular traditional restaurant is Bosduifklip, built around a rocky outcrop between Lamberts Bay and Clanwilliam.

Lamberts Bay has truly established itself as a holiday destination. At its modern hotel all the bedrooms either face the sea or the swimming pool, and it

*Above left: The man-made bird hide on Bird Island, Lamberts Bay*

*Above right: The view from the bird hide on Bird Island at Lamberts Bay*

*Above left:  Muisbosskerm open air restaurant on the beach front outside Lamberts Bay*

*Above right:  The propeller of the HMS Sybille in the garden of the Sandveld Museum in Lamberts Bay*

offers a choice of guesthouses. Attractions include visits to a breeding station for the small Sandveld tortoises, the Sandveld museum, or the old buildings and bird sanctuary at Van Puttensvlei, the first farm in the area. Alternatives include boat trips to fish for snoek (of the barracuda family) or just watch the dolphins and whales at play. One day we will have to come back again. The fishing may even be better than at Strandfontein!

## Graafwater

The last stretch of road takes us back to the route taken by the early explorers from the Cape. We follow the Clanwilliam tarred road and turn north at Graafwater, travelling past Heerenlogement to Vredendal. Unlike other towns that can trace their roots back to important historical milestones, whether it be peaceful, exciting or bloody, Graafwater's origin is somewhat mundane. It was set up in 1910 as a railway siding when the railway line was built from Cape Town to Klawer. The passenger trains used to pass this spot at night and although it might have stopped to take on water, none of the passengers were actually made aware of its existence. Today it is a pleasant town catering for surrounding farmers at the foot of the Cederberg mountains, and a stopover for tourist trains during the flower season of August and September or to the nearby Boschenbach Nature Reserve.

---

### Graafwater
All business facilities
Hotel, full range of accommodation
Traditional cuisine restaurant

**Attractions:**
Historical sites, Heerenlogement
Hikes
Boschenbach Game Reserve
Flowers in spring

*Above left: Heerenlogement overhang and zinc blockhouse from the Anglo Boer War period*

*Above right: Graffiti on the Heerenlogement rock dating back to 1712 and 1783*

It was also on the route of the early explorers. Groups under leadership of Pieter van Meerhoff, 1661, Oloff Bergh in 1683 and Simon van der Stel in the 1685 must have passed through, or close by the current Graafwater. One of their popular stopovers was at Heerenlogement north of Graafwater. We stop next to the farm house and climb the low ridge to the rock overhang, now a national monument. The earliest graffiti on the cave walls date back to 1712, but luckily the walls have been fenced off so no new graffiti can be added. From the elevated spot you can see quite a distance and the shelter offered by the cave together with the clear view, explain why this site was popular.

Nearby is a zinc blockhouse which formed part of the defence line erected by the Cape Government during the 1899 to 1902 Anglo Boer War. This part of the western coast saw very little military action, except for the 'naval battle' at Lamberts Bay, which is most probably one of the reasons for the survival of the blockhouse.

\*     \*     \*     \*

# Recipes that stood the test of time

It is easy to list unique South African dishes and cakes such as bobotie, koeksisters, beskuit, biltong and snoek. But are these dishes and recipes also unique and tested along the western coast of the country? The answer must lie in the origin and reason for these dishes.

The climate along the western coast is hot and dry. Food had to last and not be affected by heat. The meat, mostly sheep and goat, was often stringy and tough. Milk was available, if not from cows, then from goats. But fresh vegetables were rare and limited to long-life produce such as pumpkin, squash and dried pulses. Rain was too sporadic to allow grain crops to be grown, and the flour, maize, rice, sugar and pulses were all bought in bulk. Successful cooking and baking therefore depended on the following:

Slow cooking of meat over a low heat to ensure that the result is tender and tasty,

Dried beskuit, or rusks and cookies that will last,

Soups made from meaty stock, pulses and edible plants (like sorrel) or vegetables.

Of the popular recipes that stood the test of time, there are numerous recipes available, each one with a small twist claiming to be the secret. But to be honest, the secret of local dishes lies in the process of cooking rather than in the recipe, and can therefore be updated to today's lifestyle. Here are a few trusted recipes that have been adjusted over the years and stood the test of time.

## Green Bean Stew (Bredie)

The secret lies in the slow cooking over a low heat with a small amount of water. Traditionally this was made with brisket, but any meat will do provided it has some fat and bone, like chops, rib or brisket, cut to single portions. Braise a few roughly chopped onions in a little oil, butter or fat, remove and when very hot, sear the meat quickly on all sides. Add only one cup of water to the pot, and salt, pepper and spices to taste. Some common spices used include a few whole cloves and laurel leaves. Cover the saucepan and simmer for at least 3 to 4 hours. Check occasionally to ensure that there is still water in the pot and top up to the one cup when necessary. Around one hour before the meal, add a few peeled and roughly cubed potatoes, and a quarter of an hour later enough sliced green beans for the meal. The meat by this time should be brown and tender in a delicious brown gravy. Scoop any excess fat from the sauce in the pan. Dish up with rice and vegetables to taste. Peeled and quartered tomatoes can be used instead of the beans to make a tasty tomato bredie.

## Koeksisters

Koeksister, Afrikaans for cake sisters, is an all-round South African favourite. It is really a doughnut, formed into plaits and dipped into a medium syrup, but the secret lies in the syrup and method of deep frying. Prepare a medium syrup of two cups of water, four cups of sugar, the juice of half a lemon and a cinnamon stick if required, the day before you plan to make the koeksisters. Keep the syrup in a saucepan in the fridge to remain cold.

The next day, prepare a doughnut mixture, roll out to about two cm thick and cut into blocks of 8x3 cm. Cut two lengthwise slits in each block and plait the three strands. Drop the koeksisters gently into the hot oil, not more than six at a time, and deep fry on both sides until golden brown. Remove with a scoop, drain off excess oil, and immerse immediately into the ice cold syrup. Stand the syrup in a shallow ice-filled pan to keep it cold. Submerge the koeksisters in the syrup for a few seconds, remove and place on a grid to allow excess syrup to drain.

## Skuinskoek

Skuinskoek must be the one truly original western coast recipe as I have yet to find it anywhere else. Prepare sweetened bun dough, preferably made with yeast and flavoured with aniseed, similar to the Afrikaans mosbeskuit (must bun). Allow the dough to rise, press lightly to a thickness of approximately three cm and cut into parallelogram slices, hence the name skuinskoek or angled cake. Deep fry in hot oil until cooked and sprinkle with caster sugar if preferred.

## Roosterkoek

Roosterkoek is really only bread or scone dough flattened to the size of a slice of bread and slowly grilled over the coals. The dough can be placed on the cooler edges of the grid iron while the meat is grilled in the centre. Turn regularly until cooked and serve with butter. This is an excellent alternative to bread, easy to make and absorbs the flavour of the barbecued meat.

## Beskuit

Another old favourite, beskuit, or rusk, is like roosterkoek, modified bun dough, baked and then slowly dried in a cool oven. Mix your favourite bun recipe, but add extra butter and sugar to give it a richer flavour and texture. Form into small buns, crowded together in the baking tin.

Once baked, let them cool and then break each bun into fist size or smaller chunks. Spread the chunks on a baking sheet and leave overnight in a cool oven (50 to 80 degrees) until fully dried, hard and crispy. Beskuit can be eaten as is, but is best when dunked in tea or coffee.

## Melkkos

This is a favourite with children and a convenient last minute meal. Prepare a pasta dough of flour, egg and water and roll out as thinly as possible. Cut into very narrow strips and sprinkle with flour to keep the strips separated. Drop the strips into boiling milk without lowering the temperature and simmer until thickened or the dough is cooked. Serve in soup bowls and sprinkle with a sugar and cinnamon mixture, consisting of one cup of sugar and one teaspoon of fine cinnamon.

## Biltong and bokkoms

Although not worth making yourself, the other two old favourites are biltong and bokkoms. Biltong are strips of meat rubbed with salt and coriander and then dried in a cool airy room, Bokkoms, also referred to as the Namaqua biltong, are herrings which are heavily salted and dried, sold in bunches and eaten by peeling the dried flesh off the bones. Both of these make fine savoury snacks between meals.

# 4. Kamiesberg

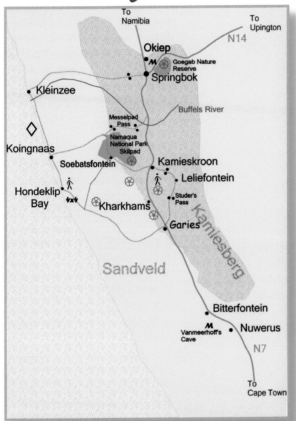

**Northern Cape Tourism Authority**
15 Dalham Road, Kimberley 8301
Tel: +27 (0)53 832 2657
Email: tourism@northerncape.org.za
Website: www.northerncape.org.za

**West Coast Regional Tourism Organisation**
PO Box 242, Moorreesburg 7310
Tel: +27 (0)22 433 2380
Email: tourism@capewestcoast.org
Website: www.capewestcoast.org

**Namakwa Tourism Information**
Voortrekker Street, PO Box 5
Springbok 8240
Tel: +27 (0)27 718 2985/6
Email: tourismbk@namakwa-dm.co.za
Website: www.northerncape.org.za

# 4. Kamiesberg

We are on our way and join the N7 again at Vanrhynsdorp. As we cross the last of the Knersvlakte to the north, and knowing the secret of the bleak plains, the struggle and victory of the plants in their fight for survival, we are able to view the scenery with respect and understanding. We pass the turn-off towards the succulent trail farm and the sign for the Ratelgat and Luiperskop Griqua Development Centre before the Knersvlakte gives way to the mountainous Hardeveld closer to our first stop at Bitterfontein. About 20 km before Bitterfontein we pass Nuwerus to the left, a small village and, in South African terms, only a stone's throw from its neighbour, Bitterfontein.

## Nuwerus

Like Vanrhynsdorp and Vredendal, a long standing rivalry existed between Nuwerus and Bitterfontein. Nuwerus, directly translating to 'new resting place', dates back to the period after the first

---

**Nuwerus**
Limited business facilities
Guesthouse

**Attractions:**
Historical site (Vanmeerhoff's Cave)
Flowers in spring

---

railway link to Klawer around 1915. The postal service from Klawer and Vanrhynsdorp to the north established its first stopover on the farm Aardvarkgat. A name translating into eater's hole was not acceptable and the stopover was renamed Nuwerus. It received formal recognition when the Dutch Reformed Church acknowledged Nuwerus as a separate congregation in 1921 to service all of the Hardeveld region, including Bitterfontein. A church, school and large boarding house, for children from surrounding farms, were built, and Nuwerus grew.

During the early 1920s however, drought and economic hardships forced many farmers and residents in the area into bankruptcy. Various deputations were made and for the first time, the parliament approved a scheme requested by the local member of parliament to extend the railway line from Klawer. This approval was unique, as the decision was not based on sound economic principles, but to offer employment to the destitute. The question was however where the terminus should be and the route the line should follow.

A logical choice would have been to extend the line from Klawer to Nuwerus via Vanrhynsdorp. Both these towns were well established and the railway line could have followed the flat Knersvlakte, making it relatively easy to construct. The decision however went in favour of Bitterfontein via Vredendal, through the lower lying river valley, thus bypassing and marginalising both Vanrhynsdorp and Nuwerus. We already know the

*Above: The desalination plant and salt pans outside Bitterfontein*

impact on Vanrhynsdorp, but Nuwerus and Bitterfontein compromised a bit better. The line was completed in 1927 and Bitterfontein built a hotel, while Nuwerus retained the church and school for the area.

## Bitterfontein

We stop at the Bitterfontein hotel for a drink. On the wall of the lounge are several group photos of rugby teams, which Johanna comments on with some awe.

'Oh those!' the manager responds. 'They are the photos of our winning teams from 1994 to 2003.'

---

**Bitterfontein**
All business facilities
Hotel and guesthouses

**Attractions:**
Historical site (Vanmeerhoff's Cave)
Granite Mining
Flowers in spring

---

After further prompting, we manage to tease out the full story. This combined Bitterfontein and Nuwerus rugby team consists mainly of young farmers who get together to play the matches in the local league. Because of the distances they have to travel, they seldom, if ever, have the chance to practice as a team in between matches, and yet they have been the league champions for nine years! Johanna is very aware of this, because the cup final usually has to be played at Vredendal, often against Vredendal!

Bitterfontein, though not much more than the hotel, a few shops and the station, harbours a few interesting facts. The name is, quite literally, derived from the fountain of bitter, really brackish, water which is still the main source of water for the town. It also boasts the first desalination plant to purify drinking water for a town in the southern hemisphere. This plant and the salt pans are clearly visible from the road immediately before the turn-off towards the town, and the plant has recently linked up with Rietpoort, a nearby village, to provide them with valuable drinking water. The fresh water was also essential in the days

## 4. KAMIESBERG

*Above left:  Granite blocks waiting to be transported from Bitterfontein*

*Above right:  Granite boulders in the Kamiesberg range near Kamieskroon*

of steam locomotion to transport freight and passenger.

Today the station platform does not have, or need, a name board as the daily diesel trains are only used to transport freight, the bulk of which consist of massive blocks of blue and red granite. Yes, we have entered the granite mountains of Namaqualand. On farms around Bitterfontein granite, and to a lesser extent marble, quarries can be found. You can visit the farms, but it is worth checking before you go. Quarries close down once the granite has been removed, such as the previously famous Bitterfontein green granite site, or Kersbos, where today the only remains is a picnic area in a circle of granite rocks.

One spot where granite will not be quarried, is at Vanmeerhoff's Cave. After Heerenlogement and Fleermuijsklip, this cave used to be the next stopover site for the early explorers during the 17th century. The cave was named after Pieter van Meerhoff, one of these early explorers, and can be reached from either Bitterfontein or Nuwerus towards Meerhofkasteel. The cave walls still contain markings from the days of the early travels.

Incidents at Bitterfontein and Nuwerus are also grim reminders that we are entering the world of diamonds and diamond crimes. In 1931 Bitterfontein was the scene of one of the world's greatest diamond robberies when diamonds to the value of £80,000 were stolen from a mailbag, never to be traced. The Nuwerus incident was not so clear-cut. In the late 1940's a schoolgirl, Bettie Smith was found drowned after a flash flood. Although the coroner returned a verdict of death by drowning, rumours abounded that she was actually the innocent victim of a diamond heist. The day before her death she apparently received a parcel from her boyfriend at Alexander Bay, a major diamond mining town, and rumours abounded for years that the robbers were under the impression that her parcel contained diamonds meant for them. Especially after the capture and conviction of a suspect gang of illicit diamond smugglers a few months later, the story did not go away.

Halfway between Bitterfontein and Garies, just before crossing the Swartdoring River, we pass the border sign between the Western Cape and Northern Cape provinces. Normally this crossing will go unnoticed by the traveller, but to us it is significant, as it means we have officially entered the district of Namakwa, and more specifically the Kamiesberg municipality and mountain range, an important target in our tour.

The Kamiesberg range derived its name from the Khoi word, th'amies, meaning a jumble. The Khoikhoi have always been good at giving descriptive names to places, but here they excelled. Whereas the drop from the Karoo plateau to the Knersvlakte near Vanrhynsdorp forms a sheer wall, the escarpment in Namaqualand rather resembles an archaeological dig. All the excess sand and dirt have been washed and brushed aside to reveal a jumble of massive rocks

surrounded by the rubble of discarded soil. The further north you go, the larger and more prominent these boulders become. No wonder I have always had a love for mountains, having spent my childhood years amongst these mountains and boulders.

## Garies

Garies is a typical isolated rural town, roughly on the route of the early explorers. Oloff Bergh referred to a camp, which he called 'Graspleyn' next to the 'Groene-doornbos' River in his journal of 1682 and unsurprisingly, the Khoi word for Garies is th'aries, meaning coach grass or kweek in Afrikaans. These names aptly describe the abundance of grass and green thorn trees which can be found in the riverbed of the Green River, flowing past the town. Even as early as 1779, Captain Jacob Gordon referred to the Garrisch River in his travel writing, but the actual establishment of a town is rather closely linked to religion.

During the 19th century the remoteness of the farms along the western coast of South Africa meant that members of the Dutch Reformed Church could only attend services a few times a year and had to travel far, and be away for long periods of time, to be able to get married or to baptise their children. As early as 1845 the church started evaluating suitable locations for churches and congregations in the Namaqualand

---

**Garies**

All business facilities
Hotel, full range of accommodation

**Attractions:**
Historical sites
Hikes
Flowers in spring, flower trails

---

area, including Garies. The decision of HA Rossouw, the owner of the farm Goedeverwachting, to sell his farm to Gerard Genis in 1884, heralded the birth of Garies. Genis subdivided part of his farm into plots for development and gave permission for a church to be built on his property. The church was built from 1884 to 1885 and the village developed around it. Initially the village name changed from Goedeverwachting, meaning good prospects, to Genisdal. In 1910 the name was officially changed back to Garies, the original Khoi name, by John X Merriman, the prime minister at the Cape. Gerard Genis played a leading role in the development of the town and his original shop is still operational as the information centre, a focal point for action during the flower season from August to September each year.

Noon on a hot summer day is never a good time to arrive at a sleepy town like Garies. The main street is deserted and everything is closed for the lunch hour break. We decide to make a quick detour to the local school before booking in at our hotel. The granite school building has not changed much since Johan, Johanna and I left Garies many years ago, and we spend a delightful half an hour with the school secretary. It is now one of the key secondary schools, with feeder schools from all over the Kamiesberg region. The two large boarding houses accommodate children who have to board because of the vast distances, the lucky ones on a weekly basis, but the rest with only one break per term. Here you have to learn to be self-sufficient from a very young age, it is a hard country.

*Right: Grootkop (large hill) to the west of Garies*

*Below left: Part of Garies as viewed from Letterklip*

*Below right: Garies Secondary School built with local blue granity blocks*

*Above left: Letterklip (letter stone) enforced as a defence post during the Anglo Boer War*

*Above right: The municipal camping and caravan park at Garies*

Before the N7 bypass was built in 1961, the main road from the Cape to Springbok used to pass through the town. Most of the buildings along the street are still as we remember them, although many serve different functions. The doctor's house and surgery is a guest house but the old church is gone, replaced by a new modern church. The town hall, where many plays were performed by the local drama group, became the Kamiesberg municipal offices, and the original Genis shop has been transformed into a busy information centre for flower seekers. The playing field opposite the house where we used to live has been turned into a very pleasant and well equipped caravan and camping site. Each site is grassed and protected from the sun by a sweet thorn tree and a permanent camp guard is on duty. This spot must be popular during the flower season.

Although Garies did not see active fighting during the Anglo Boer War, apart from the shops being relieved of provisions by the fighting Boer troops, Lieut. Col. White was sent to Garies from the Cape in 1901 to erect one of the defence outposts in Namaqualand. The fort they built around the set of massive boulders just outside Garies is still there as a reminder. Letterklip or letter stone, as the boulders became known, is now a national monument and contains various inscriptions, including some from the days of Col. White's commandos. We follow the sandy track to Letterklip to add to the jigsaw of events which constituted the Boer War in Namaqualand.

Garies, like Kamieskroon lies in the heart of the magnificent flower displays of Namaqualand in spring. During the six weeks in August and September the town is alive and vibrant, but for the rest of the year it lies dormant, preparing again for the next annual influx of tourists. As we deliberately did not join the throng of spring time visitors, we have the town to ourselves and decide to make the most of it. This afternoon we are following one of the popular flower circular tours, albeit without the flowers, namely the trip

*Left: Leliefontein Mission church*
*Above: View from Studer's pass*

to Leliefontein on top of the Kamiesberg range. Dave learnt his lesson the previous time we did the trip, and reduces the pressure in the tyres to allow for a slightly smoother ride over the corrugation in the dirt road. On the way we stop for a few photos, along the narrow and impressive Studer's pass and the farm on top of the pass which is a real oasis - a weekend on a farm like this would be a dream!

## *Leliefontein*

Leliefontein is the site of the oldest mission station in Namaqualand, dating back to 1816 when the Reverend Barnabas Shaw from the London Missionary Society was allowed to start missionary work amongst the Namaquas on the loan farm given to them by Lord Cathcart, the governor at the Cape. The church was completed in 1855 along a neo-Gothic style, but the vicarage, still in use, is much older. In its garden you can still see the old sundial given to the Reverend

Shaw, and the church bell was a gift from the Reverend JH George in England in memory of his father Clement George from Bebington in Cheshire, who loved to visit the mission station. Leliefontein, now a Methodist mission church, is an active and peaceful community, but also the site of one of the more bloody and regrettable incidents in Namaqualand during the last months of the Anglo Boer War in 1902.

After some mixed attempts to gain support around Calvinia and Vanrhynsdorp, General Smuts and his Boer commandos started their move towards the copper mines in Springbok. Moving ahead of the main force, General Maritz and his small reconnaissance team sounded out the residents of the various villages and mission stations to convince them to side with the Boers, or if not, at least to desist from giving food and aid to the English.

One of these visits in January 1902, was to Leliefontein where a plea for neutrality was made and rejected by the residents under the leadership of Barnabas Links. A skirmish developed between Maritz and Links, resulting in the death of Links and a narrow escape for the Boers. Maritz returned the next day to punish the community by killing more than 30 men. The residents fled to Garies and Okiep, only to return after the end of the war to a deserted and plundered village. Two plaques in the Leliefontein church, listing the names of the fallen, are the sole reminders of this incident.

## Kharkams, Darter's Grave

Immediately after breakfast we leave Garies. We want to exploit the early cooler part of the day as we have two short hikes planned - to Darter's grave and to Bowesdorp. The night before we left Vredendal, I asked the Reverend Engelbrecht for directions to Darter's grave. Very few tourist attractions in Namaqualand are sign-posted, and unless you know about their existence and exactly where to find them, you will miss out on some of the best the region has to offer. The Reverend Engelbrecht's instructions were quite clear:

Halfway between Garies and Kamieskroon, you pass Kharkams to your left,

Pass the turn-off to Hantjieskraal,

There will be a dam on your left, and then a long hill with a small house on your left,

On top of the hill you will see a wild olive tree (olienhoutboom) to your right near the road,

The grave is underneath this tree enclosed by a metal picket fence.

He was spot on, down to the fact that there is nowhere to park and we have to pull off the road as far as possible for safety. What he did not say though, is that the picket fence around the grave is not the only fence and we have to either climb over the road-side fence or take photos from the side of the road. Then why is there so much interest in this

**Leliefontein**
Basic business facilities
Camping accommodation

**Attractions:**
Historical mission station
Flowers in spring
Hikes

*Above: Darter's grave and the area where he was killed in an ambush*

65

particular grave? Lieut. CJ Darter was a member of Col. White's commando stationed at Garies. On their way to reinforce the troops in Okiep, he was killed in an ambush in March 1902. He was buried on the spot where he died and the land on which he was buried was later purchased from the farmer as a war grave. Although a popular rumour claims that it was bought by Britain and is the smallest piece of 'British soil in South Africa', it was actually obtained by the South African government. At only 128 sq m, it may arguably be one of the smallest pieces of separately registered land in South Africa, bought from JH Koegelenberg in 1906, and officially known as 'Lieutenant Darter, Portion 3 of Rietkloof No 446'.

On the way to Darter's Grave we pass Kharkams. This is one of the communal Namaqua farms set aside by the government to prevent encroaching farmers to overrun the area. The primary school services surrounding areas and the village is in the centre of the Namaqua flower region.

## Kamieskroon
All business facilities
Hotel, full range of accommodation

**Attractions:**
Historical sites
Namaqua National Park
Flowers in spring
Flower routes and hiking

# Kamieskroon

The rock formation in the Kamiesberg range between Garies and Kamieskroon is awesome to say the least. Massive boulders form artistic shapes and in between the rocks we can clearly spot some quiver trees and aloes. Kamieskroon, translated from Nama and Afrikaans means the crown of the jumble and the hill to the south east of the town, also known as Kardou, duly carries the crowned rock on its tip!

We stop at the Kamieskroon hotel for refreshments and find the manager very forthcoming. The discussion inevitably moves to the flower season and the role played by hotels during those exciting six weeks of the year. The Kamieskroon Hotel distinguished itself in the past by offering classes in photography to entice visitors during the flower season and we wonder whether it would not be a good idea for more local places to follow their example.

'You have to remember,' he responds, 'that six weeks in a year is a very short period. For the rest of the year business in a small town is slow and we have to survive until the next season comes around.'

'Why can't the municipalities help in their own way to encourage tourism? We have seen quite a few tourist brochures, but even if attractions, like Darter's grave, are mentioned, there are no directions or sign-posts to these spots and no parking

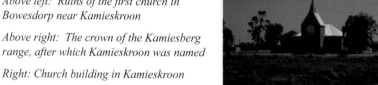

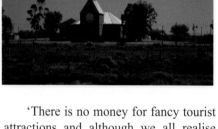

*Above left: Ruins of the first church in Bowesdorp near Kamieskroon*

*Above right: The crown of the Kamiesberg range, after which Kamieskroon was named*

*Right: Church building in Kamieskroon*

or other facilities once you manage to find them.' Johan counters.

'That would be nice and will help our business as well,' is the reply. 'However, remember that the district of Namakwa is geographically the largest in South Africa with a distance of 700 km between the northern and southern borders, and with a low population of less than one person per sq km. Furthermore, even though the coastline boasts a rich diamond trade, the riches belong to the private companies and the government - Lawrence Green appropriately described Namaqualand as "a land of diamonds and poverty". In the Kamiesberg municipality the towns of Garies and Kamieskroon are the only two with tax paying residents who have to fund all the domestic services and housing development for themselves as well as the other five smaller villages where most people still live below the breadline.'

'There is no money for fancy tourist attractions and although we all realise the importance of tourism, we have to do the best we can. However, if you would like to know what to look for around Kamieskroon, I can certainly help.'

And help, he did. The history of Kamieskroon, like many of the other places, is fascinating and linked to the Church. When in 1864 the Dutch Reformed Church council decided to establish a congregation and build a church in the Kamiesberg area, the choice fell on a protected ravine between granite outcrops on the farm Wilgenhoutskloof, willow ravine. A church and school were built and the village called Bowesdorp, named after Dr. Henry Bowe, the local district surgeon, developed. Whereas the ravine provided the necessary protection, it was too narrow to offer much scope for expansion and by 1924 the situation was so dire that the church council decided to move. The church was abandoned in favour of a new building at the nearby site of Kamieskroon, followed by the school, police station, post office and the shops. Bowesdorp became a ghost town, and deteriorated until only some ruins of the old church are left in the valley.

The Dutch Reformed Church in Kamieskroon still occupies centre stage in the town and during the flower season the church hall transforms itself into an information centre and tearoom where tourists can find out where the best flowers can be viewed, can relax with tea and cake, or buy local arts and crafts. We stop at Bowesdorp on our way north and visit the ruins amidst a flock of grazing sheep and goats. The ruins are surely spooky but impressive, as are the towering granite mountains surrounding the narrow valley.

Like Garies, Kamieskroon has some of the best flower displays during spring, and offers circular tours to these spots.

## Hondeklip Bay
Basic business facilities
Self catering and camping

**Attractions**
Crayfishing
Hiking and scenic drives
Shipwreck
Flowers in spring

One, which overlaps with Garies, is the trip to Leliefontein, but this time via the Kamiesberg pass, which is even more impressive than the Studer's pass. As we have already done this route from Garies, we decide to make a detour towards the coastal region before continuing to Springbok. All of this is dirt road and after a short delay to reduce the pressure in the tyres, we are on our way.

The road winds through bouldered koppies spotted with quiver trees and past the turn-off to Skilpad. The name of the farm used to be Skilpadgrouwater, Afrikaans for 'water dug up by a tortoise', with an interesting tale attached. The Namaquas trusted the ability of the local tortoises to survive where no one else can, and when they saw a tortoise digging for water, they followed suit and found a reliable source of water near the surface. Skilpad became famous for its display of daisies in spring and in 1988 The World Wildlife Fund (WWF) of South Africa established a wild flower reserve on the farm Skilpad in an attempt to conserve the wild flowers of the region. The reserve is open during the flower season when you can be assured of a sea of orange daisies.

After Skilpad we have a choice. We either continue to the coastal village of Hondeklip Bay, or turn back towards Springbok. Time is however against the visit to Hondeklip Bay and we take the right turn past Soebatsfontein, through the Namaqua National Park and the Messelpad pass on the way to Springbok.

*Above left: Skilpad Wild Flower Reserve in spring*

*Above right: A built-up section in the Messelpad between Springbok and Hondeklip Bay*

# Hondeklip Bay

The route all the way from Springbok to Hondeklip Bay or dog stone bay, has an interesting history linked to copper. The commercial mining of copper started in 1852 near Springbok and immediately raised the same problem that Simon van der Stel encountered, namely how to transport the metal to the nearest port. Two possible harbours were identified, at Hondeklip Bay and Port Nolloth. Of the two, Hondeklip Bay at that stage offered the best prospects and the road, including necessary passes along the way, was built. One of the mountain passes on this route is the Messelpad pass, named for the sections where the embankments of the road had to be constructed with local granite, using the typical dry stone-wall masonry technique. A team of convicts did the building work and the ruins of their jail can still be seen in the valley of the Buffels River next to the road.

Copper was transported by ox wagon to Hondeklip Bay and shipped from there until the early 1870s when the harbour at Port Nolloth was completed and a railway line linked the copper mines to its port. This meant that the masonry work on the road to Hondeklip Bay stopped and the port reverted back to being a fishing village, and for a short period of time, a fish and crayfish canning centre.

Now Hondeklip Bay it is a small fishing village with the usual licensed individual diamond dredgers working along the coast. It has a caravan park and a few shops and offers 4x4 trails and crayfish diving during the season. A licence can be obtained from Garies or Kamieskroon. South of the village is the wreck of the Aristea that ran aground in 1945 and near the police station you can see the dog shaped rock after which the village was named. Unfortunately one of the ears of the dog was apparently hit by lightning and broke off!

## Soebatsfontein and the Namaqua National Park

After the turn-off we drive past Soebatsfontein. The name translates into 'pleading fountain' and is linked to at least two stories. One story claims that Dutch sailors pleaded for their lives from the San at the fountain, while a more specific tale is that a goatherd named Hendrik Stievert, was killed at the fountain by San hunters in 1798 despite pleading for his life. A few kilometre further along we reach the Namaqua National Park, a 60,000 ha park including the Skilpad Reserve. It is the first Parks Empowering People Project in South Africa, proclaimed in May 2003 Although still under development, it features a resource centre, ablution and picnic facilities. It is popular for flowers in spring, succulents all year round, and the Namaqua tortoises, the smallest species of tortoise alive.

We follow the winding road through the rocky outcrops, stopping now and then for photos of the quiver trees and aloes flowering amongst the rocks. There are also succulents that we recognise from our visit in Vanrhynsdorp or from past experience, like the trailing stems, wedge like leaves and fleshy fruit of the suurvy, or sour fig (Carpobrotus edulis), which we ate as children, and the botterboom or butter tree (Tylecodon wallichii) which we used as a sledge for sliding down the granite boulders to the horror of our parents who had to deal with the green stains on our pants!

The next part of the road takes us over the Wildeperdehoek pass or the corner of the wild horses, and the Messelpad pass. This is where we pick up the afternoon peak traffic. At least four 4x4 trucks pass us at a much faster speed than we are willing to travel. They are obviously employees of the diamond mines at Koingnaas off to Springbok for a long weekend!

The one site we missed by taking the detour to Soebatsfontein, lies between Kamieskroon and the turn-off to the Messelpad pass north of the Buffels River. To the right of the N7 near the river bed is the old milkwood tree under which Adam Kok, the Griqua Chief used to assemble his tribal heads before moving and resettling in Griquastad near the Gariep during the 19th century. The tree is still there although not so easy to spot after the construction of the N7 as it is further away from the road.

\*       \*       \*       \*

The trip took longer than we planned, and highlighted one of the problems in leaving the beaten track in Namaqualand. Both the mobile/cell phones of Johan and Dave have been rendered useless as we have been out of reach of mobile reception masts. We could not warn our next hotel in Okiep that we would be late arrivals. We need not have worried at this time of the year, but it is a relief to eventually arrive and relax for the next stay in the copper mining region of the western coast of South Africa.

# 5. Copper Mountains

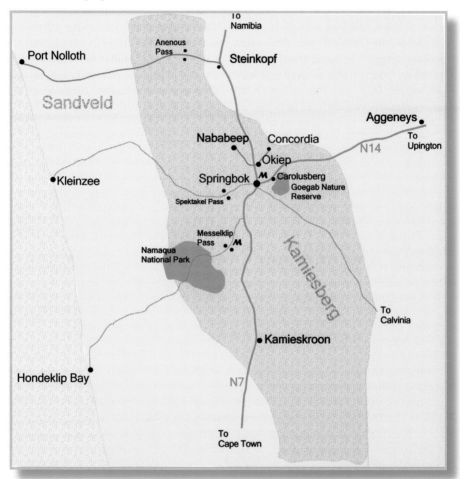

**Northern Cape Tourism Authority**
15 Dalham Road, Kimberley 8301
Tel: +27 (0)53 832 2657
Email: tourism@northerncape.org.za
Website: www.northerncape.org.za

**Namakwa Tourism Information**
Voortrekker Street, PO Box 5
Springbok 8240
Tel: +27 (0)27 718 2985/6
Email: tourismbk@namakwa-dm.co.za
Website: www.northerncape.org.za

# 5. Copper Mountains

Few events can have such a decisive impact on the shaping of a place than the discovery of mineral wealth. You only have to reflect on the impact of the 1880s diamond rush, and 1890s gold rush on places like Kimberley and Johannesburg, to agree. The western coast of South Africa is no exception, although the mineral wealth was not nearly on the same scale.

## Discovery of copper

The Khoikhoi were the first people to discover copper in the mountains around Springbok, and used it to make decorative trinkets from the ore. The Dutch, like all Europeans, searched for the wealth of the legendary Monomotapa in the 1660s but not much further than the basin of the Olifants River. The search was renewed when Khoikhoi traders brought some of the copper to trade at the Cape in the 1680s. The race for riches was on again and this time with the blessing of the Dutch East India Company (VOC). After three reconnaissance trips to find a suitable route to the copper mountains, Simon van der Stel set out on 25th of August 1685 with a seriously large party of:

fifteen ox wagons
eight carts
a carriage
a boat
350 oxen
thirteen horses
eight mules
56 members of the VOC Company
46 drivers
Khoikhoi translators, guides and a few slaves.

Detailed diaries were kept by the governor and his appointed scribes like van Meerhoff and Hendrik Claudius. Known resting places included Heerenlogement, Fleermuijsklip, Vanmeerhoff's cave and the banks of the Green River near Garies. On the 21st of October 1685 the party reached the copper mountains near Springbok. They sank three shafts and extracted some ore to be sent to Holland for analysis. The VOC in Holland deemed the ore to be of poor quality and combined with the remoteness and inaccessibility of the mines the dream of riches was put on hold for the next two centuries. The only reminders of this attempt are the diaries and the mine shafts, one of which near Carolusberg, five kilometres east of Springbok, has been declared a national monument.

## A copper roller coaster

In 1852 commercially viable copper deposits were discovered on the farm Melkboschkuil, not very far from where Simon van der Stel prospected for copper in 1685. This time the find was significant

*Above left: The reason why the first copper mine was known as the Blue Mine*

*Above right: The historical smoke stack and pump house in Okiep*

enough to attract prospectors and fortune seekers and the Namaqualand copper roller coaster ride started, developing towns and villages, and changing the region for ever.

## Springbok

Phillips and King Mining Company, later to be renamed the Cape Copper Company, purchased the mining rights from the Cloete family on Melkboschkuil and started the first commercial copper extraction at the site. Prospectors and fortune seekers flocked and settled near the only fountain with drinkable water at Melkboschkuil and a village was officially laid out for the miners in 1862. Springbok, or Springbokfontein, named after the buck frequenting the fountain, was born.

## Nababeep

Other mines were sunk during the 1850s at Concordia and Nababeep, drawing some of their workers from the mission stations at Concordia and Steinkopf. When the Cape Copper Company established its head office and a smelting plant for the production of copper at its mine in Nababeep during the 1860s, another new village was planned and developed by the company. To retain key personnel, Nababeep received all the necessary services, including schools and churches, but Springbok was still the leading copper town in the area.

The copper market collapsed in the early 1860s and only the strongest mining companies survived, including the Cape Copper Company at Nababeep and Springbok.

## Okiep

During the 1870s rich copper ore was discovered north of Springbok near Okiep. Fickle miners left the already flagging mine in Springbok and mounted an exodus to Okiep. As in the case of Springbok and Nababeep, Okiep was established in order to house miners and took over as the leading mining town from Springbok.

When the Okiep mine flooded in 1873, the Cape Copper Company ordered pumping engines from Cornwall and two were installed during the 1870s and 1880s with the help of more Cornish tin miners. The Cornish beam pump and the adjacent smoke stack for its boilers are now national monuments in the centre of Okiep. Okiep flourished as it turned out to be the richest copper mine in the world while the Springbok mining activities slowed down and the mine closed in 1888.

### Port Nolloth and Hondeklip Bay

Transport was a problem. Hondeklip Bay and Port Nolloth were evaluated as suitable ports to export the ore, and Hondeklip Bay was the first port to be selected. The building of the Messelpad pass between Springbok and Hondeklip Bay was commissioned in the 1860s to assist the transportation of the ore by ox wagon over the mountains. Work also started on the construction of a railway line between the copper mines and Port Nolloth.

By 1876 the harbour at Port Nolloth and the railway line between Okiep and Port Nolloth were completed and copper transportation to Hondeklip Bay ceased, as did the construction of the Messelpad pass. It was Port Nolloth's turn in the limelight.

Initially the train between Port Nolloth and the copper mines was mule drawn. Father Simon who made the trip in 1882 on his way to Pella, gave a graphic description of the journey. The train consisted of 30 cars with two mules and two conductors each, one conductor to speed on the mules by whip, and the other to work the brakes on the downhill sections. The journey took all morning to reach the bottom of the Anenous pass, the afternoon to ascend the pass and after a sleep-over on top of the pass, another day to reach Okiep. Steam locomotion was only introduced in 1890.

### 1899 to 1902  War interlude

Wars are often fought around wealth and possessions, one party to increase its wealth and the other party to defend and protect its own possessions. So it was with the Anglo Boer war of 1899 to 1902. The British Cape Colony issued an ultimatum to the Transvaal and Free State to peacefully surrender their rights over the gold and diamond mines, or to fight. They chose to fight. The western coast of the Cape Colony was far removed from this battle zone and already in the hands of the British, so in theory unaffected, that is, until 1901 when General Jan Smuts proposed to invade the Cape via Namaqualand. One of his main targets was the copper mines around Springbok. Colonel White was sent from the Cape to set up a defence line along the western coast, but in April 1902 the Boer commandos made their move in the copper region.

The three forts around Springbok were attacked and conquered within three days. The Boer commandos turned their attention to the other mining towns.

*Above left:  Nababeep copper mine*

*Above right:  Clara, the steam locomotive used to transport copper to Port Nolloth*

These towns were mainly defended by the home guards and employees of the mining companies. The home guard at Concordia, owned by the Namaqua Copper Company, surrendered without a single shot being fired and General Smuts moved his headquarters to Concordia, north of Okiep. The fortification around Okiep however consisted of 15 forts built under the direction of Major Dean, the manager of the Cape Copper Company, and he used more than 20 km of barbed wire as deterrent in between. Fort Shelton between Okiep and Concordia was the headquarters for this home guard.

The siege of Okiep started on the 3rd of April 1902, but the villagers held on. There was even an episode on the 28th of April when two members of the Boer commando, accompanied by a white flag, apparently challenged the home guard to a rugby match. After some debate the request was denied for fear that the invitation was really a front to spy on the railway timetable. The Boers did try to blow up the railway line on the 1st of

May, and the home guard could have been right in their assumptions. Fortunately this all happened during the dying days of the war as General Smuts already had to leave Concordia via Port Nolloth on the 26th of April for the final signing of the peace treaty. The Boer commandos withdrew from Springbok on the 2nd of May and Okiep on the 4th of May 1902. It was a short war - a mere interlude in the annals of the copper mines in Namaqualand.

## Springbok fights back

The copper market collapsed again after the first World War and in 1919 the Cape Copper Company stopped mining operations at most of its mines and discontinued exploration by 1922.

Springbok, the leading town, was not dependent on mining anymore. In 1922 it received village status and municipal status in 1933. The extension of the railway line from Klawer to Bitterfontein in 1924, brought the Cape market a little closer and for a while the South African Railways obligingly ran a passenger and transport bus service between Bitterfontein and Springbok to support this remote region of the country. Money was however at a premium during a worldwide depression, and by 1930 even this transport service was stopped. The roads were in a terrible state and the towns north of Bitterfontein became cut off and neglected.

History however did not reckon with the resourcefulness and determination of the people of Namaqualand. The residents of Springbok asked the owners of a local garage, Joe Jowell and Jaap du Plessis, if they would be willing to provide transport to Bitterfontein to pick up essential provisions for the town. They agreed and Jaap du Plessis personally converted an old Buick into a freight carrying truck.

It was a wonder that this first trip was uneventful as the demand for provisions was so high that they had to drastically exceed the freight carrying load of the vehicle! This trip heralded the beginning of Jowell's Transport business, built around the need for personal and business transport, especially mining, throughout the whole of the north-western Cape. The company flourished, was quoted for the first time on the Johannesburg Stock Exchange in 1955 and is now quoted as TRENCOR with interests all over South Africa and overseas.

As an example of the quality of people in this part of the world, Joe Jowell, despite a serious heart complaint, built up the business and in addition was:

Member of the Springbok town council for 34 years, of which he was mayor for 27 years,

Member of the Namaqualand District Council for 20 years of which he was chairman for 12 years,

Chairman of the Board for Roads and Transport,

Chairman of the Motor Dealers Association of South Africa,

Chairman of the Car Industry Association of South Africa,

Chairman of the Northwest Cape rugby union; and more.

## Nababeep again?

By 1936 the copper price recovered after years of depression. Okiep Copper Company, financed by the Americans, obtained the mining rights from the Cape Copper Company. They reopened six mines, three mills and the smelter. It retained its headquarters in Nababeep and continued to transport copper to Port Nolloth. The railway line and steam locomotives remained operational until the late 1940s and early 1950s when the company discontinued and demolished the railway line. Clara, the last steam locomotive used on the line is still on display in the mining museum at Nababeep. Jowell's Transport which was by now fairly well established, transported the coal for the steam engines from Bitterfontein and later the

*Above left: Springbok situated in the Copper mountains*

*Above right: The Springbok Lodge*

copper ore to Bitterfontein. The area was back in business, with another reversal in the relative sizes of the towns. By 1961 Nababeep was the largest town in Namaqualand with a total population of around 6,500, mostly employees of the company, compared to Springbok's population of only around 3,000.

## Balance

By this time Springbok however cemented its role as the leading diversified business town of the area. It remained the seat of the Namakwa District Council and is today not only a striving vibrant town, but the largest in Namaqualand. Nababeep is still the largest mining town and Okiep became a residential area for the neighbouring towns, and a tourist resort.

New and modern mines have since developed, like the active Carolusberg copper mine east of Springbok, and the modern copper, zinc, silver and lead mining complex at Aggeneys, 100 km east of Springbok.

\*　　\*　　\*　　\*

Reliving the history of the Copper Mountains around Springbok can already occupy us for a few days, but we find that there is more to experience in the copper mountains than history. Dave chose the Okiep Country Hotel when he did the bookings over the internet four months earlier, specifically for the pool facilities it offered to guests. To his dismay he now finds that they meant a pool table for billiards and not a swimming pool! The garden, covered in mesh to keep insects away at night, is however a reasonable substitute as we really only need a relaxing area to meet in the evenings after the day long excursions to all the sites.

## Springbok

Springbok sprawls around a klipkoppie, the same hill where one of the forts was destroyed during the Anglo Boer War. Our first stop is the Tourist Information Centre housed in the old

## Springbok

Full modern business facilities
Hotels, full range of accommodation
Restaurants

**Attractions:**
Historical buildings and museums
Historical mining sites
Goegab Nature Reserve
Flowers in spring
Hiking, 4x4 trails

Anglican church, next to the post office. The church dates back to 1861 and is the second oldest church building in Namaqualand after the mission church at Leliefontein. As we found when visiting other information centres along the route, the staff are totally professional and very helpful, and we leave with a stack of brochures, books and useful tips of what to view, where to go and when.

In the town there are other historic buildings and sites and we visit the first Dutch Reformed church built in 1921 with the traditional granite blocks and still in use; the Namaqualand museum housed in the old Jewish synagogue; and take a trip and short hike to see the Blue mine, the first commercial copper mine of the area. By now it is time to head back for lunch at the Springbok Lodge. The Springbok Lodge warrants a special mention. Not only does it provide full accommodation including a good restaurant, but offers many self catering units. After lunch we admire its display of local art; photographic and geological exhibitions; and the extensive stock of books that cover the needs of the most discerning tourist and visitor. What impresses me is that it also owns and sponsors museums, publications and events about tourist attractions in Springbok and the surrounding areas. This is something sorely needed in the remote and cash strapped region along the north-western coast.

Before heading back to our hotel, we visit the historical mine sunk by Simon van der Stel in 1685. It is more difficult to find the mine than we expected. We know that it is near the Carolusberg copper mine, but as the route is not clearly sign-posted, I misdirect the cars to a spot which looks right to me but turns out to be other old, or even recent, small shafts near the current active mine. Luckily we find the shaft on our way to the nature reserve.

Like the Ramskop Nature Reserve at Clanwilliam, this is not the best time of year to visit the Goegap Nature Reserve, southeast of Springbok. The spring flower season would have been better, especially for the Hester Malan Wild Flower section. The 15,000 ha reserve does, however, offer other attractions like game spotting

## Nababeep

All business facilities
Hotel

**Attractions:**
Mining museum
Hiking
Flowers in spring

*Above left: Granite hills and boulders on the way to Nababeep*

*Above right: The historical pumphouse in Okiep as seen from the hotel*

for the 45 species of mammals including springbok, gemsbok and the Hartman mountain zebra. For the active visitor there are hiking, mountain biking and 4X4 trails to experience.

## *Nababeep*

After breakfast the next day, we leave for Nababeep and the mining museum, followed by an afternoon at leisure. I thought we have seen the best of the granite boulders along the N7, but as the road dips down into the ravine which encloses Nababeep, I find that I have been mistaken. The name Nababeep comes from the two Nama words, 'naba' meaning the hump of an animal, and 'bib' meaning a small spring. The hump must have referred to these massive boulders!

The mining museum gives an interesting insight into the history of mining in the area, but it is really Clara, the last steam locomotive, parked outside the main building, that interests us most.

The ore was initially pulled by mules along narrow gauge line from Okiep and Nababeep to the top of the Anenous pass. From here the carts were allowed to free-wheel down the pass and then pulled again over the flat Sandveld to the harbour at Port Nolloth. On the way back the empty carts were dragged up the pass by mules. Even after switching to steam locomotives in 1890, the process of free-wheeling down the Anenous pass and pulling the carts back up by mule was continued until the railway was discontinued during the 1940s.

## *Okiep*

Johan, Janey and Johanna are spending the afternoon in Springbok for some shopping, Dave and Paul are enjoying a well deserved rest and I decide to wander around Okiep with my camera.

The name Okiep was derived from

## Okiep

All business facilities
Hotel and guesthouse

**Attractions:**
Historical sites and buildings

---

the Nama word U-gieb, meaning 'great brackish spring'. It was established as a mining town and the significant role it played during the copper boom and the Boer War has been covered in detail earlier in this chapter. We have been fortunate that the main tourist sites in Okiep are right next to the hotel, and I can easily explore the historic smoke stack and Cornish beam pump in its stone building. The smoke stack was built as a ventilation shaft in 1880 and the pump was the second to be installed to pump out the water which flooded the Okiep copper mine during the 1880s. Both pumps were Newcomen type engines invented by Thomas Newcomen in 1712, improved by James Watt and Richard Trevethick and built by J Harvey & Co. of Hayle of Cornwall in the late 1800s.

On a hill to the northeast of the town is the remains of the Crows Nest blockhouse, taken and occupied by the Boer commandos during the Anglo Boer War. The Okiep East mine also contains graffiti dating back to the war, written by the Cape Town Highlanders and Cape Garrison Artillery during the month long siege of Okiep.

## Steinkopf

Late afternoon we take a quick tour to Steinkopf and Concordia. Steinkopf started as a Rhenish mission station set up in 1819 for the local Namaqua tribes. First known as Kookfontein or boiling fountain, the settlement was renamed Steinkopf around 1842 when it became a Lutheran mission station. Its history was not always peaceful and the communal grave of 32 Nama children killed by marauding San during the early part of the 19th century is a poignant reminder of the event. The murder took place on a Sunday morning while the parents were attending a church service and the grave is still revered and known as Kinderlê (children lying here).

Nowadays Steinkopf is the centre of a large communal stock farming area, and provides labour for the nearby mines. However it is the joint tourist initiatives that demonstrates what can be done if a community works together. The Kookfontein Information Centre has

## Steinkopf

Basic business facilities
Self catering accommodation

**Attractions:**
Historical sites and ruins
Hikes

## Concordia
Limited business facilities

**Attractions:**
Mission station
Historical sites
Geological sites
Hikes

*Above: Orbicular diarite rock near Concordia*

information on all local sites including the Kinderlê grave, the position of lookout posts during the Boer War, the impressive Emanuel Succulent Nursery and tea garden, and the self catering resort Namastat.

You can also arrange for trained guides to accompany you on nature and cultural hiking trails, a worth while experience especially to find and view the various succulents and halfmens plants.

## *Concordia*

Although Concordia also started as a Rhenish mission station, established by the Reverend Brecher in 1852, its history was more closely linked to copper than Steinkopf. The Namaqua Copper Company operated a copper mine at Concordia from 1853 to 1933 when it sold the mine to the Okiep Copper Company. The defences of the mine was not as strong as that of Okiep during the Anglo Boer War and Concordia surrendered without a shot being fired. This allowed the Boer commanders to set up camp at Concordia for the siege of Okiep.

On our way back we stop for a visit to the Orbicule hill between Concordia and Okiep. This small hill contains some of the best examples of orbicular diarite in South Africa. This rock, originally only thought to be found in outcrops in Scandinavia, is an example of granitoid magmas separating while still in a fluid state, forming small globules within surrounding rock of a different composition. The display of circular and oval shapes in the rock is fascinating.

\*     \*     \*     \*

We really enjoyed our stay in the Copper mountains, but it will be an early night tonight. We have a busy schedule planned for tomorrow - a trip along the diamond coast, all the way from Port Nolloth to Alexander Bay. At last we will meet the real desert of South Africa.

# 6. Diamond Coast

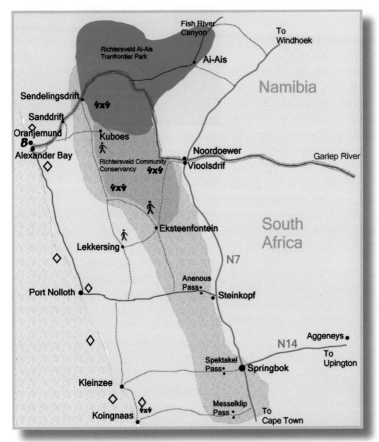

**Northern Cape Tourism Authority**
15 Dalham Road, Kimberley 8301
Tel: +27 (0)53 832 2657
Email: tourism@northerncape.org.za
Website: www.northerncape.org.za

**Diamond Coast—Forever Namaqualand**
Private Bag X01, Kleinzee 8282
Tel: +27 (0)27 807 2999
Email: nmtourism@debeersgroup.com
Website: www.coastofdiamonds.co.za

**Richtersveld Municipality, Tourism Bureau**
Private Bag X113, Port Nolloth 8280
Tel: +27 (0)27 851 1111

**South African National Parks**
PO Box 787, Pretoria 0001
Tel: +27 (0)12 426 5000
Email: reservations@sanparks.org
Website: www.sanparks.org

# 6. Diamond Coast

A few kilometres outside Okiep we reach the top of the Karoo plateau and leave the archaeological digs that are the Kamiesberg mountains, behind. It feels strange after the days of winding our way through mountains, to be able to see wide open spaces again, but this only provides a false sense of freedom. We still have to drop down the escarpment to the coast, and as soon as we reach the top of the Anenous pass shortly after Steinkopf, we descend into its ravines. The mountains in this part of the escarpment are more like rounded hills than rugged mountains and it becomes obvious why it would have been easier to build a railway line from Okiep to Port Nolloth during the 1860s rather than the more difficult route through the Kamiesberg range to Hondeklip Bay.

At the top of the pass, shaded by blue gum trees, are the ruins of the old hotel and other buildings where the rail trucks were unhooked and sent down the pass filled with the copper ore. Halfway down are the remainders of the stone shelters built to protect the line during the Anglo Boer War and at the bottom we can see the old water tank where the locomotive picked up the freight train for the rest of the journey to Port Nolloth.

The Sandveld at the bottom of the pass is a different story. This stretch of the coastal Sandveld really lives up to its name, consisting predominantly of white sea sand covered with the familiar coastal shrubs. Fortunately for us, community pressure on the mining companies had been strong enough in the past to convince them that a tarred road all the way to Alexander Bay via Port Nolloth was essential and we are spared the sandy ordeal. There is not even a need for the road to bypass obstacles, and we are faced with a straight black line, fenced on both sides with barbed wire and 'Keep Out' signs to welcome us to the diamond coast.

The first diamonds along the western coast of South West Africa (Namibia) were found near Luderitz as early as 1908. The government in the German controlled South West Africa gave the sole rights for exploration to the Deutsche Koloniale Gesellschaft (DKG) and declared the area around and south of Luderitz a Sperrgebiet, a restricted area, out of bounds to all non-mining people. All this control and secrecy was in response to the mad diamond rush at Kimberley during the late 1800s, which resulted in the 'big hole' - the world's largest man-made hole, dug by individual prospectors in search of diamonds, and the additional fear that unless the supply and price of diamonds were controlled, the flooding of the market would result in a collapse of the industry.

At least two different stories are told about the first significant diamond discovery along the Namaqua coast. The commonly accepted story is that the first diamonds were found by Captain Jack Carstens, an officer in the

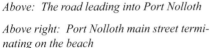

*Above: The road leading into Port Nolloth*

*Above right: Port Nolloth main street termi-nating on the beach*

*Right: Post office with its twisted pillars*

army, while visiting his parents in Port Nolloth in 1925. The Concise Illustrated South African Encyclopaedia, however, credits a man named Alberts for the first find, while he was looking for lime to whitewash the walls of a new schoolhouse near Kleinzee. Both are likely to be correct, but for the different locations as most of the small diggings were rapidly purchased by Dr. Hans Merensky. He subsequently made phenomenal finds of diamonds at Kleinzee and Alexander Bay. The cache of diamonds at Kleinzee apparently contained around 480 stones while he found over 3,000 carats of diamonds within weeks at Alexander Bay. By 1928 he convinced the South African government of the wisdom to control the industry and the State Alluvial Diggings took up joint control at Alexander Bay. The coastline from Alexander Bay to south of Hondeklip Bay was declared a restricted area.

Mining towns like Alexander Bay 1928, Kleinzee 1942, and later Koingnaas 1970, developed as closed company communities, shrouded in secrecy. All real estate in these towns belong to, and are managed by, the mining companies, down to the allocation of housing according to company status (ranch style mansions for mine managers to single sex compounds for contract workers). The coast is still very much under the control of three major mining companies. Alexkor, a semi government organisation, in the process of being privatised, controls the onshore exploration and mines from Alexander Bay to the south of Port Nolloth. Kleinzee and Koingnaas to north of the Olifants River, as well as most of the deep-sea offshore dredging operations, are under control of De Beers Consolidated Mines, while Transhex received government approval for smaller inland mining at places like Komaggas, on the banks of the Buffels

River, and the shallow coastal dredging along the coast of Namaqualand.

# Port Nolloth

Port Nolloth was originally known as Aukwatowa, the Nama for 'where the water took the old man away'. It will be interesting to know who the old man was and how come he was carried away! The name was changed to Seal Bay, or Robbebaai in Afrikaans, by the local farmers because of the numerous seals which bred along the coast, but its history as a town has really been influenced by mining, first copper and then diamonds.

It is said that when Commander Nolloth was surveying the coastline in HMS Frolic during the 1850s to find a suitable port to export copper from Springbok, he was thrown into a secluded bay by a storm. It turned out to be Seal Bay and he found his port! In 1854 work started on building a harbour and railway terminus to be completed during the 1870s. The town was officially named after Commander Nolloth in 1855. Port Nolloth was secure in its role as a copper export harbour until the collapse of copper during the 1920s. Like most coastal towns along the western coast it tried to make the most of the loss in trade by opening its first fishing factory in 1930, but it was the discovery of diamonds along the coast that gave it a new lease on life.

I was unsure about what to expect from Port Nolloth after so many guide book tales of:

'If there is such a place as "the end of the line", then Port Nolloth is surely that place', or

'Do not be daunted if an eerie mist envelopes you about 10 km from town. The weather promises eight months of gales and fog per year.'

Maybe that is why it comes as a surprise. The town of Port Nolloth today is a go-ahead town with modern shops, restaurants and all business facilities. As the seat of the Richtersveld Municipality, it has control over a vast region stretching from Steinkopf and Port Nolloth to Alexander Bay and Vioolsdrif, including the Ai-Ais/Richtersveld Transfrontier Conservation Park.

The straight road into Port Nolloth takes us past the post office with its unusual twisted columns, the municipal offices to the left, and comes to an abrupt halt on the beach. In front and to the left are a few boats and the harbour basking in the hazy morning sun, and next to the beach is the museum, housed in one

---

## Port Nolloth

All business facilities
Hotel, full range of accommodation
Restaurants

**Attractions:**

Historical buildings and museum
Mine tours
Hikes
Trips to Bird Island

---

*Above left: Boats returning in the evening mist from the day's work at sea*

*Above right: Museum in Port Nolloth with one of the original raiway coaches*

of the original pre-fabricated buildings. The only problem is the fact that it is Saturday, and as we have found in other towns, the municipal offices are closed, as is the main tourist information centre. Fortunately the museum is an alternative information centre where we can explore the history of the town and the diamond industry, and find out about attractions in the area.

Port Nolloth has one other surprise in store for visiting strangers. Approximately eight km south of Port Nolloth is McDougall's Bay, the holiday resort not only for Port Nolloth, but for the northern Namaqua area. We have actually found another Strandfontein. The resort offers holiday chalets and homes and a variety of activities such as angling, crayfish diving, bird watching trips around Bird Island, whale, seal and dolphin watching, and walks to explore the coves along the beach. McDougall's Bay could become an alternative holiday retreat to Strandfontein on our next trip.

## *Kleinzee and Koingnaas*

Although not on our route this time, it is worth while having a look at what Kleinzee, Koingnaas and the rest of the diamond coast have to offer. Both Kleinzee and Koingnaas are modern company towns with all the necessary facilities. Since the introduction of off-shore mining in the 1960s and the reduction of new on-shore diamond finds since the 1990s, there has been a slow shift in emphasis from on-shore to off-shore diamond mining. The previously closed mining towns and coastal roads linking them have been opened to allow limited tourism. This includes Kleinzee and Koingnaas, but permits are required and should be applied for at least five days in advance. Information can be obtained from the information centre at Kleinzee.

The road from Springbok to Koingnaas takes you over the Messelpad pass, and if you want to start at Kleinzee, then an equally impressive Spektakelpas, not called the spectacular pass without reason, awaits the traveller. Despite the unseemly mine dumps created by the diamond mining operations, the restricted access to the coastal region allowed seal colonies, one of which registered more than 450,000 seals, to settle along the coast, and protected the indigenous plant species from exploitation. The best way to view this pristine coastline, is to go on one of the prearranged 4x4 mining packaged tours, visiting the coastal coves, inlets and shipwrecks. A mining tour explains and demonstrates the workings of a modern alluvial diamond mine. Kleinzee also has a museum covering the mining history and a nature reserve which, although smaller in size than four rugby fields, hosts more than one hundred indigenous plant species.

---

### Kleinzee and Koingnaas
Mining towns, restricted access
All business facilities
Guesthouse at Kleinzee

**Attractions:**
Museum
Mining tours
4x4 trails

---

along the coast actually comes as a shock and disappointment as we drive from Port Nolloth to Alexander Bay. The secrecy and security which surrounded the diamond industry along the western coast of South Africa, unlike the gold mines near Johannesburg, also blocked out the reality of the destruction caused by mining activities. Diamonds are not picked up any more, but mined! Both the onshore and the offshore (sea dredging) mining processes are clearly described on the mining tours. For onshore mining the process consists of the following steps:

## Coastal Road and Mining

From Port Nolloth we continue north along the coast to Alexander Bay. Not far from Port Nolloth we pass the Muisvlak Motel, built next to an old mine dump, currently being reworked. The motel appears like a green oasis with its trees and swimming pool.

Why is it that the word 'diamond' only conjures up a shiny stone, picked up for its glow in the moonlight and embedded in jewellery, or am I alone in the delusion? The sight of the high mine dumps at the side of the road and

Prospectors drill for and pinpoint the presence of diamondiferous gravel, also known as kimberlite, usually in hollows near or on the bedrock.

The ground, or overburden, on top of this gravel is removed by heavy duty bulldozers and excavators, dumping this ground either as mine dumps next to the open cast mine, or if on the beach, then in the sea as a sea-wall.

Once the overburden has been removed, diamond deposits found in

*Above left: Checking the succulents on the way to Alexander Bay*

*Above right: The lichen field near Alexander Bay*

---

cavities are swept up and collected by hand or suction after which the gravel is excavated mechanically, crushed, washed, sifted, dried and then scanned by x-ray machines to locate the diamonds.

Finally the diamonds are picked and sorted by hand before being sold to diamond buyers for jewellery. The industrial quality diamonds are sold directly to the industry purchasers e.g. for fine drill tips.

Eventually all that is left are the mine dumps, if not used to fill the open cast shafts again. Offshore dredging on the ocean bed follows similar methods, except that the sand on the sea bed is removed by large 'vacuum cleaners' on to the boats or mobile platforms and then dumped back into the sea after the sorting.

Divers taking down the dredging pipes to the sea bed are sought after and it can be a lucrative albeit dangerous career. All the main towns like Alexander Bay have hyperbaric chambers in the event of a diver suffering from decompression illness.

Along the coastline the scenery is the same as when we first arrived at the Sandveld after descending the Anenous pass - white sand with coastal succulent vegetation, and flat. This region only receives around 45 mm of rain a year but the overnight mist along the coast offers enough moisture for the plants to survive, if not strive. Close to Alexander Bay, the signs of the Richtersveld, South Africa's only real desert, and a mountainous desert at that, unfold. Vegetation is more sparse and nearly non-existent away from the coastal belt, and mountains line the horizon.

As we approach the town, we pass an impressive sight. The hill to our right is covered by orange lichen, the largest desert lichen field in the world. The orange colour is due to the Teloschistes capensis species of lichen, also found along the coast in Namibia, but the hill is actually home to 29 different species of lichen as well as 41 species of higher plants. Apart from painting a bright spot in the otherwise bleak landscape, lichen is actually not a plant but a fusion of two unrelated organisms, algae and fungi. The fungus partner forms the body of the lichen, responsible for the absorption of moisture from the sea mist for the whole organism, and the algae's responsibility lies in the production of food through photosynthesis, again for both partners. Without roots or flowers, they propagate through spores or multiply through subdivision. Although some kinds of lichen are unpalatable to animals, lichen is sometimes referred to as the Biblical manna from heaven.

## Alexander Bay

At the entrance to Alexander Bay is the gatehouse where we have to get day permits for our visit. It is a painless process provided your passport and car papers are in order. Once through the gate, however, conflicting tourist information and confusing road signs nearly land us in trouble. I recalled the travel guides recommending the restaurant at the mine and direct Dave to the left to the museum and restaurant as per the sign-post. What the guides neglected to say is that these two buildings are in the mining sector of Alexander Bay and our on-the-spot permits do not allow us access to the mine - a fact smartly pointed out to us by an armed guard! So it means a three point turn and then following the road away

---

**Alexander Bay**
All business facilities
Guest houses and self catering

**Attractions:**
Diamond mine and museum tours
Orange River Estuary
4x4 trails
Lichen fields

---

from the sea towards the town centre.

Maybe just as well. Alexander Bay stretches out like a green ribbon along the banks of the river. You can easily forget that you are actually in a desert by just looking at the green lawns, the large proud houses and buildings lining the street. A true compliment to the support given by a mining company to its employees, or at least the ones we can see. The street ends in the shopping centre which is quite busy as it is after twelve on a Saturday and only one hour from closing time. The coffee bar has a notice in the window, offering the best coffee in the region, a claim which turns out to be surprisingly true. We are fortunate to have just enough time for an excellent cup of their filter coffee and something to eat before the doors close on us.

One interesting observation made by Paul, is that this shopping centre with its Saturday papers and discarded wrappers, is the first real example of untidiness and neglect we have come across on the tour thus far. This is actually true as all the places we have visited have been true

*Above left: Orange River Estuary with Oranjemund in the distance as seen from the golf course at Alexander Bay*

*Above right: Alexander Bay, a green strip bordering on the Richtersveld desert*

ambassadors to the region and proud thereof. Maybe if we arrived any other time than lunchtime on a Saturday we would have felt the same about Alexander Bay!

On the way back to the gate, we stop at the golf course, the highest spot, to have a good look around at the town of Alexander Bay and the Gariep River. The Gariep forms the north-western border between South Africa and Namibia and is known by various names. Gariep or Heigariep is the original Khoikhoi name meaning the grey river and is regaining its popularity. Pioneer farmers called it the Grootrivier, the largest river known to them, but in 1779 Col. Gordon named it the Orange River in honour of the prince of Orange of the Netherlands, the name still generally in use today. From our vantage point on the golf course we can also see Oranjemund, the Namibian counterpart of Alexander Bay.

## Oranjemund

Dave worked at Oranjemund for a few years and can enlighten us on its history. After the discovery of diamonds near Luderitz in 1908, most of the diamond prospecting and mining in South West Africa was concentrated there until Merensky's phenomenal find of diamonds around the mouth of the Gariep, in the late 1920s, attracted prospectors to the border. By this time South West Africa was already administered by South Africa and diamond mining was in the hands of Consolidated Diamond Mines of South West Africa (CDM), then a subsidiary company of the De Beers Corporation. CDM declared this part north of the Gariep, the Mining Area 1. They found that it contained even greater wealth in diamonds than around Alexander Bay, which mined nine million carats of diamonds between 1928 and 1995! The town of Oranjemund was established to house the employees of CDM and Dave manages to point out some of the landmarks visible from our viewpoint, including their golf course and clubhouse. In 1994, after Namibian independence, CDM was replaced by Namdeb, an equal partnership organisation between the Namibian government and De Beers. The arrangements also require Namdeb to employ Namibian residents and to give preference to Namibian suppliers. A bridge over the Gariep and border post to Namibia separate the two towns but like Alexander Bay, a permit will be needed to visit Oranjemund.

Although Oranjemund and Alexander Bay contain the world's richest deposits of alluvial, mainly gem quality, diamonds, Alexander Bay was initially linked to copper. During the 1830s Sir James Alexander mined copper at the Kodas mine not far from Sendelingsdrift on the Gariep river. He transported his copper ore by raft down the river to Alexander Bay for export, thus connecting his name to the harbour. Another source disputes this claim and contributes the name to a local trader, called Alexander, as Sir James Alexander apparently only visited the port once in 1837.

Regardless of the origin of its name, Alexander Bay is slowly transforming itself from a mining town towards long term sustainable employment and growth. Focus groups comprising members of the central and local governments and the mining companies, are exploring and developing mariculture (marine agriculture), farming and tourism as alternative industries. Mariculture projects already include the sustainable harvesting of black mussels, limpets and kelp along the coast. The Orange River Estuary, visible from our vantage point, is one of these developments. It has more than 75 species of waterbirds, the rare Barlow's lark as well as mammals such as the straw-coloured fruit bat and the Cape clawless otter. It also offers very good angling opportunities, and interesting hiking trails.

To the south and east the view away from the river paints a picture of the green town against a range of white dunes and the high Richtersveld mountains at the back.

\*     \*     \*     \*

## Attempts to diamond smuggling

Ever since parts of the western coast of Namibia and South Africa were declared restricted diamond areas, workers at the mines or casual 'prospectors' have been trying to smuggle diamonds without being caught. There are many tales of how it was tried and it is only possible to relate a few of these:

A visitor encased diamonds in a block of concrete, supposedly as an aid to support his jack in case he had to replace a flat tyre on the sandy roads. No one guessed it contained diamonds.

Diamonds were flown out, tied to the legs or body of homing pigeons sent back home from the mines. As recent as 1998 the authorities at Alexkor mine, Alexander Bay, ordered all unregistered pigeons to be shot to stop this method of smuggling. One smuggler became so confident that he overloaded the harness strapped around the homing pigeon with diamonds. The pigeon was picked up by the security police, walking along the road, too heavy to lift off!

Another thief smuggled in the pieces of a crossbow, later to shoot arrows, hollowed out and filled with diamonds over the fence to an accomplice on the other side. He was caught when one of the arrows fell in front of a security jeep.

Diamonds have been hidden in gas tanks of vehicles or in slits cut with razor blades in tyres.

Miners wedged diamonds in sweatbands or any convenient orifice. One trick used to be to hide it underneath your fingernail until safe, and then to swallow them.

On visits to a sorting office, thieves would put sticky tape on the sole of their shoes in the hope of picking up small stones which fell on the floor.

Diamonds were flown over the fence in kites or even radio controlled aeroplanes.

The heels of shoes were hollowed and re-enforced to hide diamonds when miners went home. This was not usually successful, people are x-rayed at random on leaving the secure area.

A prospector in Alexander Bay made a slit in wet biltong and inserted diamonds in the slit. Once the meat dried out, the slit closed and no one would have been able to guess that the biltong contained diamonds.

One miner broke the neck of his zither, hid some diamonds in it and sent it home to be fixed. Unfortunately his wife was not aware of his plan, had the instrument fixed and sent back, with the diamonds still in it!

However, even in the unlikely event that you may pick up a rough diamond, do not even try to keep it. The security police and Diamond Companies already know all these tricks and many more!

# Richtersveld

It is such a pity that we do not have 4x4 vehicles, because the consensus is that it would have given us a more rounded experience if we could have travelled back through the Richtersveld towards Vioolsdrif, or join up again with the road between Port Nolloth and Steinkopf.

The Richtersveld is a mountainous area south of the Gariep and the only true desert region of South Africa. When the Khoikhoi migrated south two thousand years ago, the Einiquas and Nama tribes settled here followed by missionaries,

## Sanddrift

Limited facilities, no fuel
Camping and chalets

**Attractions:**
San graves
Hiking
4x4 trails

informative brochure which I picked up at the museum in Port Nolloth, lists some of the attractions awaiting 4x4 travellers to these villages. Two routes are on offer from Alexander Bay, one leading south through the Richtersveld Conservancy region and the other northwards into the Richtersveld Transfrontier Park.

## *Richtersveld Community Conservancy*

The route to the south leads through the Richtersveld Community Conservancy region, formed in 2003 and managed by the local communities in the park. At the moment the route is suitable for vehicles with high clearance such as vans, but not cars.

### Sanddrift

Sanddrift, an apt description of the sandy low water river crossing after which it was named, is on the Gariep approximately 60 km from Alexander Bay. It is on the list of tour groups with a newly constructed rest camp for accommodation. This is one of the oldest Nama settlements and the nearby Cayman caves contain the graves of early Khoisan inhabitants, buried in a standing position, covered by buchu leaves and then piled high with stones. This is also where the legend of the halfmens tree (Pachypidium namaquanum) can be heard, according to which the original Namas who fled south from Namibia to the region, were

explorers and prospectors. Richtersveld became part of the Cape Colony in 1847 and was named after the Rhenish missionary, Dr. E Richter, who worked in the area during the 1830s.

In 1927 the Cape Government created rural reserves, including the Richtersveld, for indigenous people. The Group Areas Act of 1950 strengthened this decision by removing all intruding farmers from the trust land and forming the Richtersveld National Park to promote conservation. Since 1994 the Government has also been addressing the redistribution of wealth through the compulsory provision of housing, water and basic services to all citizens, while insisting on greater participation in the mining and other business opportunities for locals. The municipality of Richtersveld has already done much towards providing the badly needed services, and is promoting joint community projects, especially related to self-sufficiency in the production of fresh food, and tourism.

Although roads and transport are still relatively low on the priority list for development as money is scarce, an

*Right: Quiver tree, one of the desert trees along the western coast of South Africa*

### Kuboes
Limited facilities, no fuel
Self catering chalets and camping

**Attractions:**
Traditional arts and crafts
Hikes to Cornellskop, Wondergat
4x4 trails
Petroglyphs

transformed into these trees, forever longingly facing northwards to the land they had to leave behind.

## Kuboes

Kuboes, approximately 25 km east of Sanddrift, is surrounded by three mountains: the Kuboes, Van der Stel and Ploegberg mountains. Like many settlements in the north-western Cape it was started as a Rhenish Mission station in 1844 by Rev. Johan Hein who relied on Andries Domorogh, a local interpreter to help him with the language. The descendents of Andries are still living at Kuboes. It is also the only school world wide where the Nama language is taught as well as many traditional poetry, plays and dances like the Namstap. Pupils have already performed these at international level. The village has its own information centre, offers accommodation in chalets, and a traditional Nama matjieshuis resort, The Plantation, just outside the town.

A few kilometres from Kuboes is Cornellskop, the highest peak at 1,377 m. The peak, now a national heritage site, is named after Fred Cornell who prospected in this area during the early 1900s. It hosts the largest number of endangered local quiver trees (Aloe pilansii) in the world and is the location of the Wondergat or wonder hole, which according to local legend is a bottomless pit and home to the mythical Nama hero, Heitsi Eibib. A dragon-like monster snake with sparkling eyes, is apparently guarding the diamonds at the bottom of the pit on behalf of Heitsi Eibib. The fact that the depth of the hole had been measured by two geologists in the 1940s to around 44 m, does not distract from the romance of the legend as the pit was found to be water filled (another Loch Ness monster?).

## Eksteenfontein

Limited facilities, no fuel
Self catering, chalets and camping

**Attractions:**
Rooiberg Nature Reserve
Guided hiking tours
4x4 trails

A few kilometres further along towards Sendelingsdrift, in Bloeddrift, you can find a unique collection of San rock engravings of varying ages, called petroglyphs. In addition to being chipped out of rock rather than painted, these engravings differ from the normal San paintings because they include geometric designs of dots, spirals, grids and other shapes together with the normal animal shapes.

## Eksteenfontein

Eksteenfontein is situated on the southern border of the Richtersveld Conservancy region and its history,

## Lekkersing

Limited facilities, no fuel
Self catering, chalets and camping

**Attractions:**
Quartzite mine
Communal garden
Hiking and camping
Donkey cart rides

together with that of the nearby Rooiberg only dates back to the 1940s when the Rev. Eksteen started a mission on behalf of the Dutch Reformed Church for the mixed blood descendents of the Khoikhoi and Dutch, who at that stage were rejected by both groups. Today these villages offer hospitality in the community run guest houses, and guided tours in the surrounding area. The Rooiberg Guesthouse to the north-east of Eksteenfontein, used to be a mining office and walks here will, for instance, include visits to disused small fluorspar and other mining sites.

## Lekkersing

Lekkersing - sing along joyfully. The sound of the name promises happiness, and apparently referred to the bubbling sound made by a small spring on the farm of Jasper Cloete where the settlement was developed in 1926. The quartzite stone mine outside the village was established in 1964 and produces slabs of quartzite used for tiling worldwide. A communal vegetable, fruit and herb garden was started in 1999 and has already won prizes as the best garden in the Northern Cape Province - quite an achievement as it had to compete with gardens along the more fertile Gariep of the Green Karoo at Kakamas and Upington.

Accommodation is available in chalets or at a camping site at Koerdap, approximately 10 km away. Don't forget to arrange for a donkey cart ride, the most traditional way of transport in the Richtersveld.

*Above: The N7 winding through the Richtersveld mountains near Vioolsdrif*

*Right: Young halfmens (Pachypidium namaquanum) tree found in the Richtersveld mountain range*

## Ai-Ais/Richtersveld Transfrontier Conservation Park

The route from Alexander Bay to the north leads into the Richtersveld Park and is strictly for 4x4 vehicles, travelling in convoy.

With the signing of an agreement of co-operation between South Africa and Namibia in 2003, the Ai-Ais/Richtersveld Transfrontier Conservation Park became the second park to be jointly managed by South Africa and a neighbouring country. The first transfrontier park, Kgalagadi, is also on our route and is under the combined management of South Africa and Botswana. The Ai-Ais/Richtersveld park is still very much under development and therefore more the reason why a 4x4

at this stage is essential, together with enough fuel, water, camping gear and essential provisions. Temperatures can range from over 50 degrees centigrade in summer to below freezing in winter.

The 1600 sq km South African side of the park is situated in the crook of the Gariep as it works its way through and around the majestic Stinkfontein mountains and valleys with ominous names like Hellskloof, Skeleton Gorge,

### Ai-Ais/Richtersveld Transfrontier Conservation Park
No facilities
Need permit from Sendelingsdrift

**Attractions**
4x4 trails

Devil's Tooth and Gorgon's Head. The Namibian side of the Transfrontier Park includes the Fish River Canyon, regarded as the second largest canyon after the Grand Canyon in America. At this stage there is no direct road through the park to the canyon, but it can be reached from the Namibian side and a visit is worth while.

## Sendelingsdrift

Sendelingsdrift, the Afrikaans name for missionary crossing, is on the Gariep and the only South African town in the Transfrontier Park. It offers basic chalet and camping facilities, and permits for the park can be obtained form the park office. A pontoon is already in use to transport mining personnel across the river and may become an official border crossing into the Namibian side of the park in the future. All routes from Sendelingsdrift require sturdy 4x4 vehicles to explore the succulents, like the halfmens (Pachypidium namaquanum) that looks like a sentinel against the horizon with a

mop of unruly hair, and the local quiver trees (Aloe dichotoma and Aloe pilansii), or to marvel in the stark beauty of the scenery.

## Viooßsdrif

A potentially more convenient route to the park is to follow the N7 north to Vioolsdrif and then turn west. Vioolsdrif is the border post between South Africa and Namibia and was named after a resident with the surname of Viool, or violin. At this point the Gariep is framed by rocky craggy mountains which give the appearance of stacked heaps of black stones. The close proximity of the mountains can make it extremely hot in summer and temperatures of 50 degrees Centigrade are not unheard of.

When you enter the park from this direction, you have the opportunity to

*Above left and right: Pictures taken from the viewing site on the edge of the Fish River canyon in Namibia, the northern member of the Ai-Ais/Richtersveld Transfrontier Park*

## Vioolsdrif
Basic business facilities
Chalets and camping

**Attractions:**
River canoeing
Hiking
4x4 trails
Petroglyphs

acclimatise at privately owned luxury water front camping sites downstream from Vioolsdrif, before tackling some of the worst roads, but splendid scenery.

*    *    *    *

Alas, we do not have a 4x4 vehicle and the evening finds us back at our hotel in Okiep for our last night among the copper mines and Kamiesberg mountains. It is a pleasant and relaxing farewell, that is until Dave checks his mobile phone for messages. He takes his universal phone on all his travels, but as the reception along the western coast is non-existent away from the towns, he has been unable to check messages until now. Just as well as there is a weird message from William, our son, giving an urgent number for me to phone regarding my credit card. What follows is unreal.

I take the call outside so as not to disturb the other guests and there under a brilliant African summer night sky, the credit card fraud company informs me that their computer picked up an atypical spending pattern against my card. Can I please confirm whether I have made an internet purchase and a large purchase in France during the past two weeks? I laugh - it is such a world away from where we are now, and naturally agree with them to cancel the card immediately. But then the cherry on the cake - can they courier a replacement card? The fleeting image of a courier trying to catch up and finding us, is appealing, but I have to assure him that I have a second card that will get me back home! It is rude to be brought back to the reality of how small the world has become after you have been spending the past few days enjoying the remoteness and peacefulness of - - nothing.

# 7. Nama Karoo

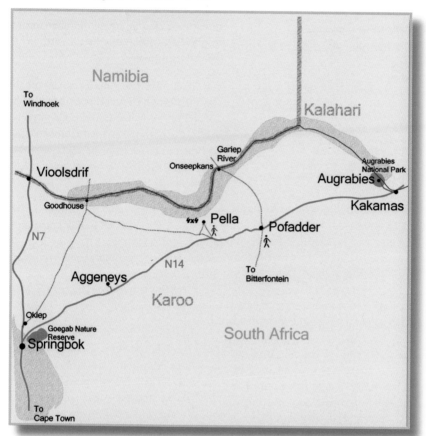

**Northern Cape Tourism Authority**
15 Dalham Road, Kimberley 8301
Tel: +27 (0)53 832 2657
Email: tourism@northerncape.org.za
Website: www.northerncape.org.za

**Namakwa Tourism Information**
Voortrekker Street, PO Box 5
Springbok 8240
Tel: +27 (0)27 718 2985/6
Email: tourismbk@namakwa-dm.co.za
Website: www.northerncape.org.za

**Green Kalahari Regional Tourism Office**
Private Bag X6039
c/o Hill and Le Roux Streets
Upington 8800
Tel: +27 (0)54 337 2800/26
Email: greenkal@bodr.gov.za
Website: www.greenkalahari.co.za

# 7. Nama Karoo

'Paul, what do you think of this kind of nothing?'

Dave's question to Paul has the ring of the rhetoric, when he suddenly realises it and adds:

'You realise that we will be able to write a book about "nothing" after this tour!'

We have just emerged from the copper mountains on the N14 from Springbok to Upington, and reached the flat Nama Karoo, when the topic turned back to 'nothing'. We know what Dave has in mind - no crowds, no traffic, nothing to interfere with the emotional enrichment of experiencing nature uncluttered by man. We surely have had ample opportunity to experience 'nothing' so far, but in the vast plains of the Nama Karoo where the past, present and future merge to become one, you can see 'two weeks into the future' and get a foresight of what the follies of today can do to that future.

Today is a travelling day. We decided beforehand not to stay over, but only to stop at Aggeneys, Pella and Pofadder and rather to push on to our next major destination, the Augrabies Falls. Two reasons influenced this decision. Firstly today is Sunday, and as we know only too well, everything closes down for the weekend by noon on Saturdays. The second reason is the heat. February is not the best month to visit the Karoo. It may be better to do some fact finding this time and come back for a longer visit in the future.

The stretch of the road from Springbok to north of Pofadder also does not inspire stopovers. It is a flat straight road, with only the fences and telephone poles as company. Farms are few, and far apart. On the horizon we can see the hues of the mountains bordering the Gariep.

The farms in the Nama Karoo, or Bushmanland as known locally, are vast and as we drive along, the reason becomes obvious. This is a part of the country where the balance between sustainable farming and a destructive desert environment is very delicate. We can pick out the farmers who are successfully rotating camps, thus preventing their livestock from destroying the vegetation. Their camps have not been grazed to the ground and still show some grass stubble before they move the flock on to the next camp with plenty of grass. In between are farms with nothing but reddish soil and stones to show for this lack of adequate farm management. You cannot help but wander how these farmers can survive the harshness of the country.

## Aggeneys
Mining town, all facilities
Guest house

**Attractions:**
Mine tours
Feral animal camp

100

*Above left: Nama Karoo plains with Aggeneys showing in the background*

*Above right: The road approaching Pella*

We follow a line of electricity pylons streaking across the open plains towards the north-west. This is interesting, as it shows how wealth, in a country with vast resources of relatively cheap fuel, is being re-distributed. OK, the installation of the electricity pylons could have been initiated by the commercial mines in these outlying regions, but government initiatives in the final years of the 20th century meant that even small villages in the remote areas are now reaping the benefits of earlier investments.

## Aggeneys

Our first stop, Aggeneys, is a modern mining town, with a large electricity sub-station nearby. The name Aggeneys means 'place of water' and refers to the spring oasis nearby. It is a modern copper, zinc, silver and lead mining complex and a typical company mining town with a paved main street, a wide range of facilities for the residents, including an eighteen hole golf course and a feral animal camp. In addition to prearranged tours to the mine, you can visit the nearby red dunes and crater, home to the red lark and other birds and animals.

## Pella

Approximately 80 km after Aggeneys we reach the turn-off to Pella. Pella was founded in 1814 by the London Missionary Society to work with a group of Khoikhoi who fled south from rival tribes in Namibia. The missionaries called the oasis Pella after the ancient Palestine town which became a refuge for persecuted Christians during the siege of Jerusalem by Titus in 70 AD. This part of the country was, however, dangerous for small groups as it was mainly inhabited by disgruntled San and Khoikhoi who resented being driven out of their previous domiciles. When the minister and his family were murdered, the Society abandoned the station, leaving the site and buildings unoccupied for the next fifty years.

In 1869, Father Gaudeul and Brother George realised that the end of the copper mining operations in Springbok also meant that their flock moved away. They heard about the abandoned buildings near water at Pella and, after negotiations with the Government, started the first Catholic mission station for this region in 1872. Initially they used the original rectory as a chapel and school, and only a small building as residence.

In 1883, Fathers Simon and Ceyte decided to build a new convent for the sisters, with the sole help of an 'Encyclopedie des Arts et Metiers', which Father Bécoulet brought with him from France two years earlier. After some near catastrophic errors, like collapsing scaffolding, and a chance discovery of top quality lime on their property, they completed the four roomed building the following year. Their work at Pella was however hampered by the custom of their congregation to move away with their livestock for a large part of each year in search of water and grazing, leaving the priests alone at the mission station. A visit to Pella by Bishop Leonard from the Cape in 1886 helped to reverse this trend. He convinced the Government of the need for a semi-funded school and boarding facilities at Pella. This allowed children and the elderly to stay behind while the rest of the families moved away with their livestock, and a permanent settlement started to develop.

Encouraged by the success of the convent building, Father Simon, Brother Rougelot and local assistants started on their masterpiece in 1886 - the building of a cathedral in the desert, again only with the aid of the encyclopaedia. Looking at the logistics to obtain and bring the raw material to Pella, we cannot help to admire the resourcefulness and determination with which they tackled and completed the project. The list reads:

200 cart loads of sand to level the ground,

400 wagon loads of stone for the foundation,

Numerous journeys by ox wagon to transport bricks from the nearby river where they were made, carrying 500 bricks at a time,

352 bags of slaked lime for mortar from the lime kilns they built themselves,

Two wagon loads of willow wood from the river, and

One bell, a gift from France, which was sent without a forwarding address

## Pella

Basic business facilities
Guest house, chalets and camping

**Attractions:**
Historical mission station
Date plantations at Klein Pella
Hiking
4x4 trails

*Above: Pella cathedral constructed with the help of an encyclopaedia*

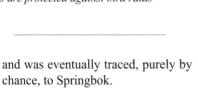

*Right: Date palms at Pella. The ripening dates are protected against bird raids*

and was eventually traced, purely by chance, to Springbok.

Even this cathedral was completed within seven years and inaugurated in 1895, and is the main attraction for our visit to Pella. The Pella Mission grew in strength and in May 1927 they welcomed the official party of the Governor General, Earl of Athlone, his wife, Princess Alice and their party on an official visit to the area. Since then they welcomed more high ranking officials and opened the Mission as a retreat to individuals or groups.

As we turn off the N14 on to the road leading to Pella, Dave has to stop a few times for me to take photographs of the unfolding scenery. Slowly the village appears against a backdrop of blue mountains, and the choice of

location seems to have been obvious, as it is difficult to find a more picturesque setting. That is, until you stop to get out of the air-conditioned car and the heat literally pushes you back into the car. We find the village almost deserted. A small group of men and boys are waiting to direct the odd traveller like us to the cathedral, at the price of a donation towards rugby shirts for their local boys' team. The priests at Pella also tend to the congregation at Aggeneys and today is the day to celebrate mass at Aggeneys. Everyone from Pella therefore piled into cars, carts and buses earlier today for the sermon and are not expected back until later.

We have enough time to look around at the cathedral and the other older buildings, some of which are now used as

*Above top and bottom: Lunch at a lay-by outside Pofadder, joined by weaver birds*

*Right: The nearby weaver bird nest. The telephone pole made up for the absence of a suitable tree for the nest*

---

local museums, and then to move on to Klein Pella. Ever since Janey heard that we plan to visit Pella on the tour, she has been determined to get hold of some Pella dates, preferably from the place itself. She and Johan used to live at Prieska, near Upington, and can still remember the boxes of plump sweet Pella dates they used to buy there.

The hot dry summers near the Gariep provide the ideal climate for dates. Gert Nienaber, for instance, built up a farm of more than 15,000 date palm trees at Klein Pella and his plantation is the largest in South Africa, drawing workers from Pella and other surrounding settlements. Alas, we forgot that it is Sunday and Janey will have to wait for her dates until we reach Kakamas.

## Pofadder

Pofadder is the name of a highly poisonous snake in South Africa, and an unfortunate name to be saddled with if you are a remote small town in the middle of nowhere. Many people in South Africa have heard of Pofadder, or know jokes about the name, but few have actually visited the town.

The name Pofadder was not actually derived from the snake, but from Klaas Pofadder, a Koranna chief who frequented the strong water spring just outside the town in addition to his main settlements on the islands in the Gariep. From these locations he often spearheaded raids against other tribes or farmers, and was eventually killed and buried at Pofadder in 1875. In the same year the Reverend Christiaan Schröder started a mission station at the nearby location of Naries, and in 1918 a town was laid out at the spring. It was initially called Theronsville, but by this time the name Pofadder had been so widely used that it stuck and later became the official name of the town. The Catholic Church built a convent and church here in 1921 and now run a chicken farm, dairy and block making business, offering employment opportunities to residents.

Pofadder is the centre of a prosperous sheep farming area, and children from the surrounding farms and smaller villages attend the local schools as boarders during the week. The flat countryside around Pofadder combined with the high temperatures in summer has its added advantage for car manufacturers who constructed a test track outside the town to test their new models.

As with the other places we visited today, the streets are deserted in the midday sun. Only mad tourists like us venture out in this kind of heat as the locals know that this is the time to relax and rest in cool curtain-drawn rooms and wait for the late afternoon before leaving the house. We stop at the hotel with its inviting pool and cool lounge, to find it closed to casual visitors on Sundays, but at least managed to get cool drinks and ice cream at the café. Outside the town we stop for a short lunch break at a lay-by underneath a tree. The lunch break eventually turned out to be not that short as there is a weaver bird nest on a nearby telephone pole and the tree is swarming with chirping little birds waiting for titbits from our table. Although we have already passed a few nests, this is our first close-up encounter with these fascinating little birds.

Weaver birds (Philetairus socius) are very social and sturdy little birds who build a massive communal nest, usually in a camel thorn tree, plentiful in the Kalahari, or else anywhere high like telephone poles, if trees are scarce. A single nest may have up to fifty chambers with openings facing the ground to keep out unwelcome predators. It can house a flock of up to 300 birds, including chicks.

### Pofadder

All business facilities
Hotel, full range of accommodation

**Attractions:**
Historical sites
Hikes

From the outside the nest resembles a thatched roof, but inside the temperature retains a comfortable range of fifteen degrees Centigrade in winter to 30 degrees Centigrade in summer. Some of the nests may also have tiny pygmy falcons as tenants. These small falcons are unable to survive the harsh winters in the desert without shelter, and as they are willing to keep away unwanted lizards and insects, the weavers tolerate their presence.

Near the lay-by we can see the rocky hills, popular for nature hikes. Quiver trees and some of the smaller succulents like the beeskloutjie (Lithops) are found here. This is also a popular bird watching spot for eagles and the red lark (Certhilauda burra). During spring, if there was enough rainfall during the winter, the flat plains are transformed into the typical flower show of daisies we have found in the rest of Namaqualand and along the coast.

\*      \*      \*      \*

From here onwards to the Gariep and our destination at the Augrabies Falls, the veld changes into more typical Kalahari scenery. You can still see for miles, but this time the ground has the reddish Kalahari sheen, covered in grass and dotted with the odd camel thorn tree. This is our entry into to the Kalahari desert, stretching for one million square kilometres over Botswana, the eastern part of Namibia and the north-western coast of South Africa.

# 8. Green Kalahari

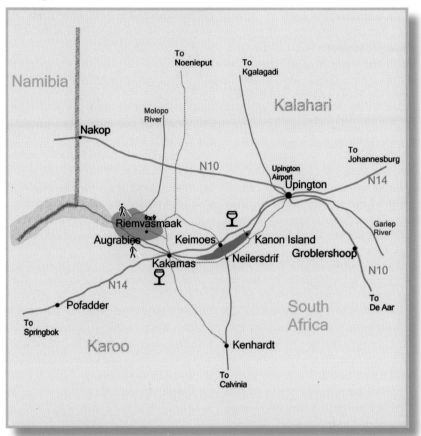

**Northern Cape Tourism Authority**
15 Dalham Road, Kimberley 8301
Tel: +27 (0)53 832 2657
Email: tourism@northerncape.org.za
Website: www.northerncape.org.za

**South African National Parks**
PO Box 787, Pretoria 0001
Tel: +27 (0)12 426 5000
Email: reservations@sanparks.org
Website: www.sanparks.org

**Green Kalahari Regional Tourism Office**
Private Bag X6039
c/o Hill and Le Roux Streets
Upington 8800
Tel: +27 (0)54 337 2800/26
Email: greenkal@bodr.gov.za
Website: www.greenkalahari.co.za

# 8. Green Kalahari

## Augrabies

Aukoerebis, the place of the great noise, and a very appropriate Khoi name for the waterfall in the Gariep River, now known as Augrabies. This is our next destination. Although well-known to the San and Khoikhoi for centuries, the first white explorers only reached the falls in the late 18th century, like Kendrik Wikar in 1778 and George Thompson in 1824 who called it the 'cataract of King George'.

Although not the highest, widest or most impressive, the waterfall has unique features which attract visitors from all over the world. Above the falls the Gariep spreads out, forming streams and islands to a width of approximately two kilometres. Where these streams converge at the falls, the effect is impressive. The river freefalls for 60 m and then drops down a further 31 m along a series of steps into a single narrow gorge, 15 km long and confined by steep granite banks rising to a height of 100 m.

It is nearly four o'clock by the time we reach the Augrabies National Park, but the outside temperature is still hovering around forty degrees centigrade. So far this has been the hottest day, and as it eventually turned out, the hottest day on the whole tour, fortunately for us! You can imagine our relief to realise that the two chalets we are renting for our stay in the park have been fitted with water cooling units. After a few minutes of rushed unpacking, each finds a suitable spot near the cooling unit and collapses until it is cooler outside.

The 25,630 ha Augrabies National Park was proclaimed in 1966 after some lengthy bargaining with the government and electricity companies who wanted to use the falls for the generation of hydro-electricity. The park offers 60 self-catering chalets and three swimming pools. The central building contains the offices, a well equipped shop, take-away meals, a ladies bar and a la carte restaurant. There are camping and picnic facilities for casual visitors.

It is the pool that first attracts Dave once he manages to surface after this chill-out session in front of the cooling system. Dave is always keen on a swim wherever and whenever he can find a pool, but today he has company. The only one not willing to give up the cool chalet for a pool, however refreshing, is Paul but

---

### Augrabies National Park
Basic business facilities
Chalets, camping accommodation

**Attractions:**
Waterfall
Hiking
Water sport
Scenic drives
Game watching

---

*Above left: Waters of the Gariep River forced through a narrow slit at the top of the Augrabies Falls*

*Above right: The canyon below the falls and one of the viewing platforms*

the rest of us are having the splash of our lives. This is the ideal cure for hot days like today and afterwards we are ready to prepare the usual evening braai on the outside dining and cooking facilities provided by the park. I especially like the clamped dustbin patent they have, whereby the bin and lid are firmly held in place by movable pipes allowing you to lift the lid by hand, but preventing any wild scavengers from tipping or opening the bin. The outside facilities are great in the evenings and I am sure Dave is enjoying the chance to cook again after the nights in hotels.

After dinner it is story time while we watch the colours of the granite rocks along the river changing in the twilight. There are the stories about the early days of the falls before they erected strong fences around the rocks, and the people that slipped and fell into the gorge by moving too close to the edge. Many of them died, but one Scandinavian who apparently survived, had all his clothes stripped off by the force of the water before being rescued.

There are also stories about the floods which used to occur every 20 to 30 years, when the thundering noise was audible as far as 40 km away. During these periods the two kilometre spread of the river above the falls could extend to five kilometres, and water would rush into the gorge not only down the waterfall, but from all around the rocks. The last major flood, in 1988, even destroyed a footbridge which was built over the ravine to offer a better view of the falls. But with civilisation also comes the taming of nature, and these floods are likely to be something of the past. The construction of the massive dams in Lesotho and along the Gariep and Vaal Rivers has tempered the flow of the river.

As the night progresses, the stories move on to myths and legends and back to the San and Khoikhoi. Similar to the 'wonder hole' at Cornellskop in the

Richtersveld, the 'bottomless pit' at the foot of the Augrabies falls is believed to contain a fortune in diamonds, washed down the river from the Kimberley diamond fields. Quite a few futile attempts were made to recover these diamonds, but the legend lives on. The great snake with diamonds for eyes still guards the treasure pot for Heitsi Eibib, the Nama hero. The powers of the snake over people are supposed to be vast. If you believe in, and respect the existence of the river monster, you will be blessed with good fortune throughout your life, otherwise if you are a disbeliever, you will suffer ill health and early death. Maybe the pythons of this area, able to grow to a length of over six metres and good swimmers at that, formed the basis for the legend.

Another legend is about the poisonous lizard that only appears late at night, searching for children not yet asleep, to bite to death. Again, this is a story to ensure the children do not stay up too late, but could have been based on the local greenish water leguaans which can grow to one and a half metres in length.

The next morning we are up early and ready for some excursions around the park. The first stop is the waterfall lookout post on the rocks. Further drives take us to the Moon Rock, a massive granite boulder rising, like a smaller version of the Australian Uluru out of the ground, and then on to Echo corner and other lookout points for views of the canyon and the river deep below. Although we are leaving the hiking trails to the younger generation, especially this time of the year, the park also offers a three day Klipspringer hiking trail and other shorter routes around the park, ravines and potholes, as well as night time game drives with a ranger. The energetic can even participate in white water rafting below the falls with private activity companies.

There is game in the park, but we did not come here for the game viewing although we did see steenbok, ground squirrels and lizards. We have added a more urgent item to our tour.

## Riemvasmaak

---

**Riemvasmaak**
Limited business facilities
Chalets and camping accommodation

**Attractions:**
Warm water spring
Hiking
4x4 trails

---

I have never even heard of Riemvasmaak, Afrikaans for 'fasten the strap', until we arrived at Augrabies. The name and history of this neighbour to the Augrabies National Park however provide a strong enough incentive to find out more and include it in the tour.

To trace the origin of the name, the story takes us back to GA. Farini,

*Above left: A chalet with its outside dining and braai area at Augrabies*

*Above right: Two local inhabitants at Augrabies, a male (colourful) and female flat lizard*

famous escape artist and author of the book 'Through the Kalahari Desert', in which he described the lost city of the Kalahari. The book inspired at least 25 further futile explorations to find this city. In 1885 Farini and his son attempted to draw the first detailed map of the Gariep around the Augrabies falls. They named many of the cascades and canyons, and even called the area the Hundred Falls. These names did not stick, but one name is supposed to date back to this period, the name Riemvasmaak. The Farini party apparently attempted to explore the 'bottomless' pit at the foot of the falls and made a raft from logs covered with hide, to float on top of the pool during the search. To lower this raft down the treacherous cliffs, they joined up all their available ox hide straps to form a 130 m rope, hence the name Riemvasmaak.

During the period 1870 to 1930, the South African Government proclaimed and set aside large tracks of land to allow Khoikhoi descendants to continue with their communal farming without interference from the encroaching land owners. Riemvasmaak or Bokvasmaak (tether the goat), as it was then known, was surveyed and declared one of these reserves in 1870 and leased to interested parties. The residents of Riemvasmaak were of diverse ethnic origin, including Damara, Nama and Herero refugees from Namibia, and Xhosas from the Transkei. They were mainly communal goat and sheep farmers.

After Namibian independence in 1974, the South African Department of Defence zoned a part of Riemvasmaak as a military training area and resettled the residents back to Namibia, Transkei and other nearby locations. Together with the Parks Board the military managed Augrabies and Riemvasmaak as a wilderness park, while also using Riemvasmaak for military training. In 1994 the original residents however launched the first successful land claim in the new political arena of South Africa.

Together with the Parks Board and the Augrabies National Park, the inhabitants are now working towards the conservation of their land and promoting parts of it for controlled tourism.

Riemvasmaak covers the part where the Molopo River joins the Gariep from the north. The easiest accessible site is the natural hot water spring where there are furnished chalets for overnight accommodation but you should bring your own linen and utensils. Similar to the villages in the Richtersveld, members of the Riemvasmaak community offer home made traditional meals and local entertainment on request. The main attractions are the 4x4 and hiking ecotrails through the river beds and the surrounding Kalahari.

This visit to the Augrabies and Riemvasmaak parks has given us a foretaste of our main destination on the tour, namely the Kgalagadi Transfrontier Park north of Upington. But before then, we head back to civilization along the banks of the Gariep, in the Green Kalahari. We leave the Augrabies National Park towards Kakamas, Keimoes and Upington with a feeling of dé ja vu, we surely have been here before! The green belt of trees, crops and especially the vineyards remind us of the Olifants River valley and how irrigation can transform a desert. The main differences lie in the geography around the Gariep and the recorded history of the area.

\*       \*       \*       \*

## The last frontier

From Upington to Augrabies, the Gariep spreads out, forming smaller sub-streams around islands. This phenomenon is at its most distinct around Keimoes, where there are more than 120 islands in the river - an ideal place to live or hide if necessary.

Around 2,000 years ago the Khoikhoi moved south from their original home in Botswana in search of new pastures for their livestock. They settled for a while at the spot where the Gariep and Vaal rivers converge, but according to their oral history, a major quarrel in the ranks led to a split-up into three subgroups. The Koranna remained at the Gariep, the Namaquas split and moved west and south-west to occupy the beaches along the western coast of South Africa and north into Namibia. The Einiquas moved west along the Gariep. The Koranna traded amicably with the neighbouring black tribes like the Sotho and Xhosas and life progressed relatively peacefully next to the river, interrupted only occasionally by the arrival of European explorers during the late 1700s.

The middle of the 19th century saw a renewed interest in the Gariep, but this time not as a point of departure, but as a final refuge. Namas, Sothos and Xhosas fled there from warring tribes in their homelands of Namibia and Transkei. San and Khoikhoi tribes moved back from the encroaching white farmers in the south, and

*Above left: The original vicarage of the Olyvenhoudtsdrift mission station, later Upington*

*Above right: An original irrigation canal and tunnel dug by hand next to the Gariep*

renegade white and mixed race individuals or groups were looking for places to hide on the numerous islands in the river. By 1870 the main tribes along the Gariep were the Griquas who moved with their chief Adam Kok from Namaqualand to Griquastad, and the Koranna tribes under the leadership of Klaas Lukas (Upington), Piet Rooi (Keimoes) and Klaas Pofadder. Renegades also used the islands near Keimoes as hiding places. Kanoneiland for example owes its name to a sustained barrage of canon fire by the government forces aimed at the island during the second Koranna war along the river. After this Klaas Lukas realised the value of literacy and invited the Dutch Reformed Mission Church to start a mission station on the farm Olyvenhoudtsdrift in 1871. The Reverend Schröder was sent to build the first church, school and vicarage on the location that will later become Upington.

In 1882, an event occurred that would change life next to the river for ever. A freed slave, Abraham September, was given a small-holding near the mission station and next to the river.

Here he demonstrated that it was possible to divert a small stream from the river to water crops, and that the desert soil around the river was fertile enough to grow crops. This was the beginning of irrigation which became the lifeline for the Gariep and the Olifants River. The settlement at Olyvenhoudtsdrift grew and was renamed Upington in 1882 in honour of Sir Thomas Upington, the resident prime minister at the Cape Colony. By 1889 Schröder extended his mission work to Keimoes and a village developed there as well.

Near the end of the 19th century, the Dutch Reformed Church held discussions with the Government on a project to help destitute white farmers who lost everything through droughts and hardships. In 1898 the first of the white farmers were allowed to settle on the farms Soetap and Kakamas, in a settlement called Bassonsdrift, although the name later changed back to Kakamas. It was here that irrigation really started. The farmers, against all advice from engineers, built their own canals by hand from a side stream of the river, under the guidance of the self-taught engineer Japie Lutz. They even dug tunnels through rock where necessary. Piet Burger perfected the water wheel to raise the water level in the canals. Some of the original canals and at least nine of the water wheels are still operational.

After these pioneering feats, the Gariep irrigation area, or the Green Kalahari as it is known today, grew from strength to strength. In 1912 a hydro-electric plant was built at Kakamas, housed in a building in the style of an Egyptian temple. It was the first hydro-electric plant in the southern hemisphere and produced enough electricity not only for Kakamas, but also for Upington and surrounding settlements, and lives on as a museum.

The impending First World War in 1914 also saw the construction of a railway line from De Aar to Upington at a rate of more than one mile per day in anticipation of a German attack from Namibia. The attack actually took place in 1915 and the graves of fallen German soldiers are in the cemetery outside Kakamas.

The railway line allowed access to a wider market and by 1927 the first fruit, oranges from the farm of Pat Sexton, was exported from Keimoes. In the 1970s the South African Dried Fruit Co-operation and the Orange River Wine Cellars Co-operation were formed, both actively supporting the farmers along the banks of the Gariep River.

\*       \*       \*       \*

Our journey for today is quite short as we plan to restrict it to the Green Kalahari. It should give us enough time to explore the towns along the way to Upington, the third major town on our tour after Vredendal and Springbok.

## Kakamas

Similar to many of the colourful town names of the region, there are more than one theory on the origin of the word Kakamas. One story is that it was derived from a Koranna word meaning poor pastures or 'the place of the raging cow or buffalo'. Apparently, either the cattle, fed on poor pasture, turned on the herdsman forcing them to cross the river at this spot, or people were attacked by buffaloes at the crossing. Another explanation links the word to a Khoi word gagamas meaning brown, the colour of the clay found in the area, and used to adorn the Khoi women.

---

**Kakamas**
All business facilities
Hotels, full range of accommodation

**Attractions:**
Historical sites and museums
Wine Cellar
Fruit Co-operative
Hikes and river sport

*Above left: Raisins from the vineyards along the Gariep on drying floors and drying racks*

*Above right: A waterwheel still operational next to the main street in Keimoes*

Nowadays there are no raging cows or buffaloes and the brown colour of the clay has been covered by green vineyards, orchards and lucerne crops.

Although we have seen how raisins are being prepared in Lutzville, we do not have to search for raisin production farms, we pass quite a few between Augrabies and Kakamas. Some farms are using both methods of floors and racks to dry their sultana grapes into delicious large soft raisins. We also stop at the Kakamas branch of the Orange River Wine Cellars, the largest co-operative cellar in South Africa. Its head office is in Upington, but we are fortunate to be able to visit the Kakamas and Keimoes branches on our way to Upington and stock up for our visit to Kgalagadi.

On our way through Kakamas we stop at the Egyptian style hydro-electric power station near the turn-off to the town centre, to visit the museum, but are even more interested in the constructed canals, water wheel and the weir built during the early days of irrigation. One of the original canals, dug and built by hand, is next to the N14 on the way to Keimoes. Another interesting spot to visit is the Neus weir along the rockery route towards Neilersdrif. The weir, the first of this specific design to allow run-off water to flow gently into the surrounding countryside, is over 900 m long and six metres high.

Kakamas has been the seat of the municipal offices for the Kai !Garib Municipality since 2000, supporting towns and villages, including Kakamas, Keimoes, Kenhardt, and Kanoneiland.

## Keimoes

I found two meanings for the name of Keimoes, the next town along the river. The traditional Khoikhoi meaning is apparently big eye, possibly referring to the fresh water spring near the Catholic Church. The alternative meaning is mouse nest in Koranna, presumably after a colony

*Above: The old mission church, now a craft shop and information centre in Keimoes*

of mice living in the area when the Koranna chief Klaas Lukas established a settlement in the area. The latter could however also refer to the 120 plus islands comprising the town. Today most of these islands are inhabited and linked by a network of formal road bridges and informal hanging foot-bridges. For that matter, the children attending the school at Klipeiland or stony island, have to walk to school across one of these hanging bridges, a somewhat daunting experience when the river is in flood! Some islands like Kanoneiland and Skanskop island are reminders of the times when fighting raged here to rid the area of some of the renegades hiding on the islands. Kanoneiland is the largest of the islands and despite its dubious past, is fully cultivated today.

We stop for lunch at Johanna's daughter, Mari and her husband Johan Botha, who have the grocery store in the main street and after lunch they take us to the other sites around Keimoes. Next to the main street is one of the water wheels on the canal, and the old mission church that gave rise to the existence of the town.

The large camel thorn, or prayer tree we pass on our way to Upington is the tree under which church services used to be held during the early years.

The visit to the nearby Tierberg Nature Reserve towards Kenhardt turns out to be a highlight. No more tigers around, but the 160 ha reserve is home to springbok, and it is especially the track leading to the top of the hill which I like. From the top we have an excellent view of the Gariep Green Kalahari belt and can see how the river spreads out at this spot.

# Upington

When Dave tried to find a hotel in Upington, all the popular hotels were fully booked and the only accommodation he could find was in a Le Must hotel residence on the banks of the Gariep. What a surprise it turns out to be. The residence is in one of the old colonial mansions, in its own magnificent sub-tropical garden

*Above left: The garden of the Le Must Residence next to the Gariep River*

*Above right: Evening relaxation on the banks of the Gariep*

with pool, and refurbished along the style of French hotels.

The tour to date has been informative and fun most of the time, but at this point we are facing mutiny. Within ten minutes of arrival, Dave and Paul announce that they are not moving from the hotel, until we check out again in two days time, and the rest of us, though relatively keen to visit the sites of Upington, are talking about tomorrow rather than this afternoon. Being a residence, the kitchen is self-service, including a honesty bar. We order

## Upington
Full modern business facilities
Hotels, full range of accommodation
Airport

**Attractions:**
Historical buildings and museums
Wine Cellars and Fruit Co-operatives
River sport
Kuierfees (visiting festival)
Spitskop Nature Reserve

dinner from the main restaurant for the evening and settle in for an afternoon around the pool, overlooking the river and Die Eiland (the island), the holiday resort directly opposite us. What an idyllic spot to relax and watch the magnificent sunset over the river.

Upington developed on the farm Olyvenhoudtsdrift when Klaas Lukas, the Koranna chief, invited the Dutch Reformed Church to start a mission station in 1871 and to teach his followers to read and write. It was renamed Upington in 1885 after Sir Thomas Upington who was the prime minister at the Cape at that time, and is today the major town of the north-western Cape, housing the offices of the Siyanda District Council and the //Khara Hais municipality.

Feeling refreshed after an afternoon of total relaxation, we leave Dave and Paul at the hotel the next morning and head towards the tourist sites. It is actually easy to reach most of them as they are close together in town. The old mission church, church hall and vicarage, built in the 1870s and 1880s have all been converted into museums about the local history. Especially the vicarage, which has been furnished in the period of the late 19th century, and the church hall where replicas of Khoikhoi and San huts are on display, are very interesting.

The final stop at the museum is in the shop at the Kalahari Dried Fruit and Coffee Shop, selling produce from the South African Dried Fruit Co-operative, the Orange River Wine Cellars and other local produce, including some very unusual ones like witblits with a mopani worm in the bottle (South African tequila?). We have already stocked up at the Orange River Wine cellars and opt for some of the dried fruit to take along to the game park.

In the grounds of the shop and in front of the police station, a short distance further along Schröder Street, are two statues of animals which played key roles in the history of the region: one of a donkey driving a cotton gin and the other of a mounted camel used by police for border patrols in the desert at the turn of the 20th century.

The rest of the day we spend on Die Eiland holiday resort and back at the hotel. Die Eiland boasts a kilometre long lane of more than 200 palm trees planted in 1935, one of the longest and densest palm tree lanes in the southern hemisphere. It is popular not only for casual day picnics next to the river at a small charge, but also to stay at the resort for a longer holiday. How easy it is to forget that we are actually in a desert!

Upington has all the shopping and business facilities expected from a prosperous commercial town, while still retaining its traditional market town traditions like the annual Raisin festival, complete with floats, fairs and performances. The main event, however, is the annual Kalahari Kuierfees or visiting festival, during October when parts of the town are transformed into open air flea markets, and local businesses offer their display rooms for visiting and local performers. This is the time to visit friends

*Above left: The palm tree lane on Die Eiland*

*Above right: Memorial statue of a donkey gin next to the church museum in Upington*

and family, sample the local produce of the region or participate in the various river sporting events specially staged for the festival, like canoe races, swimming, and many more.

The tourist brochures refer to one intriguing individual buried in Upington, namely Scotty Smith, 'the Robin Hood of the region'. Scotty Smith is another example of the dubious characters who made the Gariep their home a century ago. By the British colonial government he was branded as a bandit, highwayman, cattle thief and buyer of illicit diamonds. To the German colonial government across the border in Namibia he was an inciter of murderous attacks by the Khoikhoi, determined to rid Namibia from German influence. But to the locals he was generous and a legend. He died in Upington during the flu epidemic of 1918 and was buried there. The inscription on his gravestone aptly reads:

'George St. Leger Gordon Lenox. Gone but not forgotten. Never will his memory fade.'

However it is on the way out of Upington the next morning that we pass two of the outstanding landmarks of Upington, namely the Spitskop Nature Reserve, and its airport. To quote the ACSA (Airports Company South Africa) website:

'Upington Airport, located in the Northern Cape, boasts a 4,900 metre long runway, the longest in the African continent. Long enough to land a space shuttle, the runway was built in 1975 in a record seven months.'

When the Portuguese withdrew from Angola in 1975, South Africa lost the last refuelling stop it had in Africa and had to plan for alternatives in case it lost refuelling rights at Ila do Sol as well. Upington was a logical choice, close to the west coast and at a suitable altitude.

The runway was built long enough to comfortably land a fully loaded Boeing 747 and the airport is still used today to train Air force and Airways pilots, as well as the pilots for the South African presidential jet. For the rest of the time it is a small but busy airport, especially for transporting freight to and from the Green Kalahari and to fly in passengers on business or leisure.

The Spitskop Nature Reserve is a game reserve approximately 13 kilometres north of Upington on the way to Kgalagadi, our next destination. Although not too many animals, it has chalets and is a good place to stay if you want a reprieve from town life. A telescope on top of the rocky hill called Spitskop provides a good view of the river and the green oasis we are leaving behind for the dry Kalahari desert.

# 9. Kgalagadi

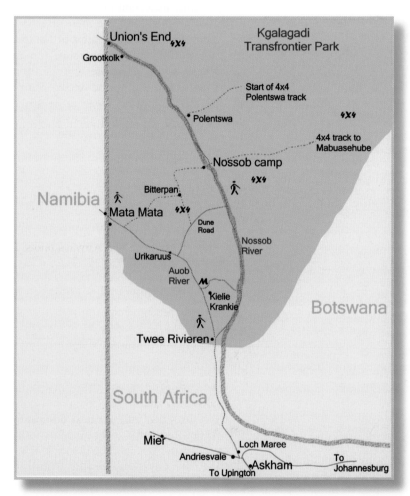

**South African National Parks**
PO Box 787, Pretoria 0001
Tel: +27 (0)12 426 5000
Email: reservations@sanparks.org
Website: www.sanparks.org

**Northern Cape Tourism Authority**
15 Dalham Road, Kimberley 8301
Tel: +27 (0)53 832 2657
Email: tourism@northerncape.org.za
Website: www.northerncape.org.za

# 9. Kgalagadi

We are refreshed and ready for the 180 km drive to the Kgalagadi Transfrontier Park, and our long awaited stay in the game reserve. We know that the road to Askham had recently been tarred, but the hair-raising stories we have read in the travel magazines about the final 60 km of dirt road, conjure up scenes of flat tyres, accidents and broken axles. Dave therefore insists on an early start to make sure that we have enough time to reach the park gate before closing time, regardless of what might happen.

We make the most of the first part of the road. Now that we are entering the true Kalahari, the differences, which we have already noticed between Pofadder and Augrabies, are prominent. The 'nothing' now consists of waves of low ridges and gullies, covered in tall grass. This part of the Kalahari is known as the dune land, and the ridges used to be red sand dunes, now mostly overgrown with

grass and low shrub and therefore less susceptible to wind erosion. The grass is a further indication that we have left the winter rainfall area and find ourselves in the summer rainfall region of Southern Africa. Rainfall here is around 255 mm a year, mainly as thunderstorms, causing sudden floods along the ditches and dry rivers, leaving the water to be soaked up by the sand within a period of days. The veld that is now green and lush, will be barren by the middle and end of the winter.

To remind us of this phenomenon, we pass a few dry salt pans, one of which has an operational salt gathering plant and the other with a tell-tale flat track of a farm road crossing the pan diagonally. I don't expect the farmers using this road are expecting the pan to be water-logged too often.

The last village before we exit the tarred road at Loch Maree, is Askham. This is also our first introduction to the memory of Roger 'Malkop' Jackson, a

*Above left: A red Kalahari dune, slowly being tamed by nature*

*Above right: An active salt pan on the way to the Kgalagadi Transfrontier Park*

*Left: The shop and garage at Loch Maree*

*Above: Friday shopping at Loch Maree*

name that will be familiar to us by the time we complete our visit to the park. Roger Jackson was a surveyor, tasked to measure out farms of around 10,000 to 13,000 ha each in the Kalahari after World War One. He named quite a few of the farms and waterholes in the park after Scottish landmarks, including Loch Maree. Rumours are that he either named Askham after the town Askham in Furness on the English Cumbrian coast, or that it came from a request for breakfast (ask for ham) or as a reference to himself (ask him). The village of Askham developed around a school and boarding house built by the Dutch Reformed church in 1931 and is still a leading village offering all the necessary assistance to travellers into the Kalahari for their vehicles and themselves.

Witdraai, Afrikaans for white bend, is only a few kilometres from Askham. It was also built in 1931, but this time to breed camels, imported from the Sudan and used to patrol the desert borders of the country. Caves at Witdraai are reminders of life during the early 1900s as they were initially used as offices and sleeping quarters for the police. Loch Maree, the farm at the turn-off to Kgalagadi on the other hand only consists of a shop, emergency garage and one house. The shop caters for the San and Khoikhoi residents of nearby Mier and surrounding farms and is well stocked with weekly prepackaged ration packs to buy. Fridays are usually the busy days for shopping here. One of the largest salt pans for which the area is renowned, can also be found on the Loch Maree farm.

We reduce the tyre pressure but the road from Loch Maree to the border turns out to be quite good for a dirt road, and apparently plans are already in place to tar this final stretch of the road to Kgalagadi as well. We reach the gate to the park around lunchtime, early enough to settle in and get familiar with the camp at Twee Rivieren before starting the serious business of game spotting.

# Kgalagadi Transfrontier Park

The game reserve was known as the Kalahari Gemsbok Park until the signing of the transfrontier agreement between South Africa and Botswana in April 1999. The name was changed to Kgalagadi, after the earlier Khoikhoi tribe who lived in this area in harmony with the San. This Kgalagadi tribe was also responsible for naming the whole region Makgadikgadi, meaning salt pan, or the great thirst, a name which became Kalahari.

After World War One it was apparent that it would be difficult to settle in these desert areas without hardship and without damaging the already delicate balance between sustainable plant growth and desert conditions. When Jackson measured out farms along the Auob river, one of the two rivers flowing through the game reserve, the farms were given to farmers free of charge on condition that they maintained the boreholes which were sunk in the riverbed for drinking water. Even with the water, the farmers still found it impossible to eke out a living

and started to kill the game for biltong to sell as extra income.

In 1931 the Kalahari Gemsbok Park was established to put an end to the destruction of the ecosystem in the region. The first game warden was Johannes Le Riche, and not only did he dedicate his life to his work, but so did his family after him, and until 1994 there had always been at least one Le Riche as game warden in the Park. On the other side of the border, Botswana reciprocated in 1938 by setting aside land for the Botswana Gemsbok National Park.

After lengthy negotiations the first transfrontier agreement in Africa was signed in April 1999. According to the agreement, the two countries would hold joint responsibility for managing the area with no formal border to prevent game from roaming freely around the 38,000 sq km of the park, of which 9,600 sq km is on the South African side and 28,400 sq km in Botswana. Management of parts of the park was also given to the Khomani San communities living in this area and the new combined park, renamed Kgalagadi Transfrontier Park, officially opened in May 2000. Most of this parkland is out of bounds to visitors - reserved for game.

## Twee Rivieren
Limited business facilities
Chalets and camping

**Attractions:**
Swimming pool
Game viewing
Guided hikes and drives

# Twee Rivieren

Twee Rivieren, the main camp, is at the southern entrance to the park and as the name implies, is situated at the point where the two dry rivers, the Auob, and the Nossob, meet. These typical

*Above:  Chalets at the Twee Rivieren Camp*

*Above right:  A ground squirrel accepting nuts at the camp*

*Right:  A black backed Cape fox scrounging for food at the camp*

ephemeral Kalahari rivers only flow for short periods of time during exceptionally good rainy seasons and only flood once every eight to eleven years. If it had not been for the water holes sunk by Roger Jackson, even the hardy desert animals would have suffered.

The camp at Twee Rivieren has modern water cooled, stone clad chalets, a well stocked shop, information centre, restaurant and to Dave's delight, a swimming pool. As in the case of Augrabies, the chalets have been designed for outdoor living, with a spacious stoep and outside braai facilities, ideal for the long evening meals and relaxation.

We spend the afternoon visiting the shop and admiring the excellent photographs and project displays in the information centre. Photographs donated by visitors and friends of the park, not only demonstrate the high standard of photography, but portray a poignant insight into the hidden animal world of the park. Lions and cheetahs with their young, with their prey, and fending off scavengers; buck in numbers or singly; and the adorable mongoose families including the meerkats; all against the brilliant red, green and blue colours of the park or dramatic thunder clouds.

As the evening draws in, we have a chance to meet the locals, two ground squirrels in search of titbits. We know we are not supposed to feed them or any other scavengers, but the temptation is just too great especially as they are tame enough to accept nuts from the hand. Later in the evening we have another guest, a black-backed Cape jackal sneaking around the braai area in a hope that we have left something to collect. This time he is not as fortunate as he was expecting to be.

## Auob and antelopes

Soon after breakfast we leave for our first day outing into the park, following the Auob to Mata Mata on the border of Namibia. Every five to ten kilometres along the road is a waterhole in the riverbed and as the speed limit in the park is 20 kph we have plenty of time to look out for animals and birds. The first game we encounter is a herd of approximately fifty blue wildebeest on the way to the waterhole just outside Twee Rivieren.

With its pronounced hump, long black mane and curved horns the individual animal looks more fearsome than the peaceful grazing herd collectively. The blue wildebeest is the one antelope in the reserve that is not really suited to dry desert conditions. They have to drink water at least every second or third day, and as a result can usually be found near the waterholes.

The next most common buck we find is the beautiful and graceful springbok, internationally familiar as the sport symbol

*Above: Grazing herd of blue wildebeest*

*Above: Springbok grazing the three thorn bushes*

*Below: A lone gemsbok in the river bed*

*Below: Red hartebeest in the river bed*

*Above left: One of the old farm houses and the waterhole which the farmer had to protect*

*Above right: Picnic at Urikaruus with only the border posts to deter the animals*

of South Africa. Sometimes we notice a herd of them at or near the waterholes, or resting in the shade of the camel thorn trees in the river bed. Sometimes we notice only one or two males on their own. We assume that these are young males kicked out of the herd to find their own way, but find a different explanation when we ask the game warden about this.

'The loner on the outskirts of a herd is not an outcast, but the dominant male. By walking ahead he demonstrates his power and warns other intruding males or predators that he is willing to fight to protect his herd. This is true for herds like springbok and blue wildebeest as well.'

This does not apply to the graceful gemsbok, the all-round favourite with us. The beautiful tan animal with the distinctive black and white markings on its head and legs and straight spear-like horns is, like the San, a true desert dweller. We notice them singly or in pairs on the dunes and as with the springbok, the game warden also has an explanation

for their solitary wanderings.

'The gemsbok is the only truly adapted desert antelope. It does not have to drink water as it can extract moisture from the wide variety of food it grazes on, including the wild melons of the desert, the tsama and other succulents. It grazes at night when the moisture content of plants is higher and excretes concentrated urine and faeces in order to retain moisture. Most remarkable, however is the vascular lining in its nose allowing it to use this as a cooling mechanism for the blood flowing to its brain, which will stay cooler than the rest of the body, even in the hot sunlight.'

## Waterholes and picnic sites

Each waterhole has a name, including some of the Scottish names like Munro and Dalkeith, reminiscent of the work done by Roger Jackson. Others again are descriptive, such as Rooibrak halfway to

Mata Mata, which conjures a vision of red rocks around the waterhole containing brackish water; or 'Jan se Draai' in the Nossob river, where a Nama, called Jan, decided that it might be safer to turn around and retreat from the desert.

Two of the water holes near Mata Mata are however only referred to as Thirteenth Borehole and Fourteenth Borehole. Their original old Dutch names were 'Groot Skrij' and 'Klein Skrij' and to quote the Kgalagadi Transfrontier Information Guide:

'The reason for the name change was the translation of the word "skrij" into English - it means "diarrhoea"! A traveller's cattle suffered this fate after eating the tsama melons and drinking the water here, and the names served as a warning to those who followed.'

At most of these holes we are lucky enough to find something, like a relaxing herd of grazing springbok, a lone fox, some meerkats or ground squirrels, a few ostriches or a large blue crane stopping for a drink of water. High up along the ridges of the river are the ruins of some of the old houses erected by the farmers who were guarding the boreholes. At Auchterlone for instance a museum is being erected as a memorial to these people and to the history of the region.

We stop for a break at Urikaruus, the only picnic site along the Auob where visitors are allowed to get out of their cars and relax in the shade of the trees. It is not a very reassuring place if you are of nervous disposition as there is no real fence around the picnic area, only a few low painted marker stones, more to keep people in than to keep animals out! Janey was telling us about her sister whose party stopped at a similar site, to find that the entrance to the ladies toilet was blocked by a lion basking in the sun. Needless to say, they did not stay long! Luckily we do not have to worry as there are workers busy improving the facilities and we can concentrate on worrying the lizards with our cameras and watching the raptors circling in the sky.

# Mata Mata

Closer to Mata Mata the excitement builds up when we spot our first giraffes. These animals are not really indigenous to Kgalagadi. A group of eight giraffes were transferred from the Etosha National Park in Namibia in 1990. They managed to adapt quite well in this corner of the park, feeding on the acacias (Acacia erioloba, Acacia mellifera and Acacia haematoxylon) that are growing here. Our

**Mata Mata**
Limited business facilities
Chalets and camping

**Attractions:**
Game viewing
Guided hikes and drives

*Above left: Giraffes only found around Mata Mata in the Kgalagadi Transfrontier Park*

*Above right: Competing for the road with a herd of springbok*

day has been successful as the only large antelope species we have not yet seen in the park are the red hartebeest and the eland.

The red hartebeest, a few of which we will manage to see the next day near Nossob, usually form small herds consisting of females, their calves, young subordinate males and the dominant male who does all the mating and guards the territory. As the name implies, the skin colour is a rich amber with darker legs and face, but it is especially the twisted horns that distinguish them from the other antelopes. This is one buck that is able to outrun a lion and is therefore fairly safe from the local predators.

We will not see any eland during our stay. The game wardens warned us that they may have moved towards the Botswana side of the park where the grazing is better. Being the largest of the antelope species in the park, up to 20 times the weight of the dainty springbok, they will be found where there is enough food to sustain them. The skin colour has

more grey with the red and the horns are straight and much shorter than those of the gemsbok. Despite their size, they are very agile and able to clear a two metre high fence from a standing position.

As we are not staying over at Mata Mata, we stop at a picnic site for lunch and have a quick look at their shop before heading back to Twee Rivieren. Like all the other camps, Mata Mata provides self catering chalets and camping facilities, but this time without a swimming pool.

Tomorrow we are leaving for the Nossob camp where we plan to stay over, and judging by our experiences today, it promises to be another exciting day.

## *Nossob and the cats*

The second river in the Kgalagadi Transfrontier Park is the Nossob, another dry river bed flowing all the way from north-eastern Namibia and through the

Kalahari. It also forms the official border between South Africa and Botswana, not that the game or even many of the visitors will notice it. It takes us a while to realise that the small whitewashed posts planted in the river bed are not milestones, but actually border posts, reading RSA (Republic of South Africa) on the one side and RB (Republic of Botswana) on the other. With the road winding in and out of these posts, we have been changing countries quite often in the time it takes us to travel from Twee Rivieren to the Nossob camp. We start out full of expectations for the day, and are not disappointed.

Hardly three waterholes from Twee Rivieren we notice a large cat resting in the shade of a tree. We stop to look and after much arguing about whether it is a leopard or a cheetah we eventually agree that it can only be a leopard, especially when it got up to walk away and we could get a better look at the spots. What a start to the day. The beauty of game parks is that when you spot rare animals, you always pass the message on to other visitors and as we are informing another couple about the sighting, they tell us that they have just left two lionesses with their cubs drinking at the next water hole.

To our delight the lions are still there, resting in the shade. The one lioness is keeping the cubs away from the road-side, while the second lioness is lying quite close to the road, presumably on guard duty! We stop for quite a while just to look and take photographs and only leave them with regret. It is a pity that they have not been accompanied by a male, but as the cubs must be around two years old, they do not need protection against other males any more and the impressive Kalahari male lion with its distinctive black mane must have moved on to find a new mate.

A few water holes further on a whole herd of springbok is blocking the road. A large tree next to the road is the reason, as it is providing the best shade in the

*Above left: Leopard walking away after a siesta underneath a tree*

*Above right: Lioness on guard while the rest of the group relax out of site nearby*

area. It looks as if the herd split itself into groups. The adults with the very young are lying peacefully in the road or next to it in the shade while the young ones are staying together, daring each other to have a closer look at the cars and us. Again we manage to get a few very good photographs and gently have to inch forward to indicate that we would like to pass. After these three exciting stops, we also manage to see a few red hartebeest and the usual wildebeest, springbok, ostriches and gemsbok.

## *Nossob rest camp*

The Nossob camp, though also equipped with modern self catering chalets and camping facilities only has a small shop and information centre at the office, but the display in the information centre is interesting and keeps us occupied while our papers are being checked.

The electricity in the camp switches off between eleven pm and five am each night and we have to plan our evening events accordingly. Tonight we have

---

### Nossob Camp
Limited business facilities
Chalets and camping

**Attractions:**
Game viewing
Guided hikes and drives

---

booked on the night drive tour through the reserve, conducted by one of the game wardens, and will hopefully be back just in time to get ready for bed before the lights go out.

If you have not been on an evening drive, the experience is worth the while. The group leaves the camp about half an hour after the gate closes for the evening and as the sun is still shining, the drive starts off with anticipation. Every so often the driver will stop the open sided truck, get out and inform us about a plant or animal we can see.

We each get a sprig of a dense growing shrub next to the road.

'This is a three thorn (Rhigozum trichotomum) bush, so called because it usually sprouts three side branches at a time, and is a typical desert plant. The leaves are very small all along the stems, but when it is dry the plant will drop these leaves and give the appearance of being dead until the next rains come. After good rains the leaves sprout and the plant flowers within a few days, to make the best of the abundance. Springbok are especially fond of its leaves, flowers and seed pods.'

At the next stop he picks a few young tsama melons to pass around.

'One of the life giving plants of the Kalahari is the tsama (Citrullus lanatus), as it often forms the only source of water during very dry periods. It contains up to 95 percent of its weight in pure water and, similar to the gemsbok cucumber

*Above left: Bus stopping for sundowners*

*Above right: A female barking gecko*

*Right: Three thorn bush and tsamas*

(Acanthosicyos naudinianus), which has a more spiky version of fruit, is eaten by many animals including buck, rodents and even jackal.'

It is nearly a disappointment when we reach the sundowner spot and are allowed to get out of the truck as we realise that this is also the halfway mark. We were asked to bring our own refreshments for this stop, and take advantage of the opportunity to talk to the guide with our drinks at sunset.

The drive back is even more exciting than the first part. The game warden gives a strong spotlight to two of the guests, one on each side of the truck. The instruction is to scan the bush on each side for animals, or even the glint of the light reflecting from their eyes. Each time someone spots an animal the truck stops, allowing us to see quite a few springhares and other smaller mammals together with

the usual gemsbok and jackals.

'The springhare, or sometimes called the South African kangaroo, is actually a rodent, built like a kangaroo with very short front legs. It is a nocturnal animal and as it is hunted by more than twenty predators, it digs a series of tunnels with quite a few entrances to hide or escape, and also breeds throughout the year to make up for losses.'

The most amazing stop is when the game warden jumps out and, after scurrying around, comes to the side of the truck with a small lizard in his hand.

'This is a barking gecko, so called because of the clicking sound the males make at dusk - you must have heard it when we stopped for sundowners. Only the males make this sound, trying to attract females to their burrows and the reason why these sounds are so clear is that the funnel-shaped burrows help to amplify the sound.'

We are not lucky enough to see any predators, but after this we need time to absorb all the events of the day, and it does not take long for the house to fall quiet.

## *Raptors and other Birds*

Last night it rained. I hardly fell asleep when the wind heralded in a storm. You know when it is a storm wind in Africa. It is accompanied by the approaching lightning and thunder (count the seconds between the lightning strike and the sound of the thunder – one second for eight kilometres), and then you smell the rain. I remember from my childhood the fresh smell of damp earth and the excitement it created amongst animals and people alike - we are getting rain, the hot temperatures will drop, and there will be new growth in the next few days! It turned out to be quite a storm and we even had to close our window for a while so as not to get soaked.

This morning the storm has gone and we are left with a fresh damp morning. Everyone is in a good mood, even the campers who had to bear the brunt of the pelting rain during the night. You can compare it to a sunny day in the UK with smiles all around. There are tracks in the damp sand in front of our chalet, one set possibly made by a jackal, another by a large blister beetle, and the third, mimicking the tracks of miniature toy

*Above: Tracks in the sand after the rain*

*Right top: Giant Kalahari millipedes*

*Right bottom: A blister beetle*

*Above left: Approach to the game viewing hide at Nossob camp*

*Above right: Blue wildebeest at the waterhole as seen from the viewing hide*

cars, must belong to the giant Kalahari millipedes which are now crawling out of their burrows after the rain. The millipedes only have man as their enemy as they produce a poisonous secretion above their legs when disturbed. It is fascinating to watch them gliding with their hundreds of pairs of feet. Apparently when young they grow by adding a segment, inclusive of two pairs of legs, at a time. The warden however warned us against the 5 cm long black blister beetle with the horizontal white line along its sides, as it is able to squirt formic acid to a distance of 30 cm, causing blisters on the skin.

After a quick breakfast we head for the hide next to the waterhole. This is one of the added features of the camp at Nossob, the fact that you can observe game at the waterhole from a well constructed hide without having to leave the camp. Large charts on the walls help to identify the birds. The more unusual birds we have spotted so far in the game reserve include a Kori bustard (Ardeotis kori) in the tall grass along the Auob, a stately secretary

bird (Sagittarius serpentarius), a few whitebacked vultures (Gyps africanus) on our way to Nossob, and a barn owl (Tyto alba) sleeping in one of the trees in the camp site at Nossob. This morning two Bateleur short-tailed eagles (Terathopius ecaudatus) have stopped for a drink. They are taking their time, firstly surveying the area from the top of a tree trunk next to the water hole and then slowly moving down to the water's edge. We watch their slow motion actions, uninterrupted by the presence of other animals. The approaching herds of blue wildebeest and springbok are still slowly munching their way towards the water.

By the time the two herds reach the water, first carefully, and then with abandon as some of the young wildebeest walk straight into the waterhole, the raptors have gone. I can understand why this hide is so popular. You can stay for a few minutes while your tour group is waiting to depart, or stay the whole day and watch the ever changing pageant around the water hole. Even if there are no

*Above left: Flowering duwweltjies, containing the sand of the Kalahari dunes*

*Above right: Weaver bird nests in a dead camel thorn tree*

raptors or game to see, there are still the smaller birds flocking around the hide and water, such as the beautiful shaft-tailed whydah (Vidua regia) birds nesting next to the hide, the common Cape sparrows (Passer melanurus), the sociable weaver birds (Philetairus socius), and many more. Along the Auob and the Nossob routes we have come across some very impressive weaver bird nests in the dead camel thorn trees.

## Dune road

On the advice of the game warden at Nossob, we take the dune road back to Twee Rivieren. He assured us that, although the name may imply a sandy track, the surface of the road is gravel and as good as the other main roads in the park. This route promises a new perspective to the reserve as it traverses the red sand dunes, each time exposing a different scene from the top of a dune.

The sand, reddened by oxide, is still very much visible and good for photography, but has been tempered by the growth of hardy semi-desert plants which are allowed to flourish in the park without the danger of over-grazing. We have already been introduced to the tsama and the gemsbok cucumber, but are now able to see how these plants manage to tame the desert.

The yellow flowers of the devil's thorn (Tribulus zeheri) or duwweltjie in Afrikaans, is well known to most of us and easily spotted as it creeps over the sand. The yellow flowers contrast well against the red sand, but don't be deceived as the seed pod is a small hard ball with sharp thorns sticking out in all directions, and quite capable of causing grief to anyone daring to tread on them with bare feet.

Other prominent plants are the black storm (Senna italica) with its fern-like leaves and yellow stalks of flowers rising up from the plant like candles, and then of course the trailing stems of the tsama plants. With fewer water holes than in the river beds, the only large antelope we see are gemsbok, but three incidents made up for the loss of game.

Twice we come across a family of ostriches. The first time, a dozen small chicks are actually running in the road, still too inexperienced to realise that it will be safer for them to leave the road. At a distance, the anxious parents are watching us with alarm. We are forced to stop both cars until the chicks have left the road as none of us are willing to incur the wrath of a grown ostrich. Dave had experience of this when one of his colleagues in Oranjemund was killed by an ostrich kick through the windscreen of his vehicle. In the second family of ostriches the chicks are older, and we can relax while watching them all racing up and over the dune.

The most amusing incident is the encounter with the little steenbok. It is the smallest buck species in the reserve, a loner, and because of its varied diet does not need to drink. While we are stopping to watch some gemsbok along a dune, I notice the rump of the steenbok sticking out from behind a bush next to the road. It is like a child's game, 'you can't see me if I can't see you'. Even as the car rolls by slowly until we can see the whole of the buck except for its head, the steenbok still does not move. We are the eventual losers and have to give up and drive away from the hiding buck.

There is so much more to see and do in the Kgalagadi Transfrontier Park, but it is with sadness that we return to Twee Rivieren for our last night in the park. As in the case of the Richtersveld National Park, we must accept that some of the more unusual camps in the park can only be reached in 4x4 vehicles, but even with our cars, if we had more time, we could have driven up to the northern Namibian border post at Union's End and the camp at Groot Kolk, the hunting ground of lions, leopards and the brown hyena, or go on morning walks with the game wardens to watch meerkats and other smaller game.

*Above left: A family of ostriches fleeing over a desert dune*

*Above right: Steenbok 'hiding' from strangers*

Quite a few wilderness camps are listed in the park brochure (4x4 only), the most enticing being Bitterpan on the South African side and the Polentswa or Mabuasehube wilderness trails in Botswana. The last two trails must be in convoy and pre-booked. In all these cases you will be alone at the unfenced camp with an armed game warden, truly at one with nature.

\*       \*       \*       \*

# African night skies

This is our last night, not only at the camp, but as a group together. Tomorrow Johan and Janey will leave us at Upington to return home in the eastern Karoo while the remaining four of us have one more experience ahead, a visit to the salt pans of the Sak River in the Karoo. After dinner we relax around the dying embers of the fire. Around us are the desert night sounds making conversation superfluous.

'Now I know there is no better place!' Johanna's comment brings back memories of how it all began, especially when she adds: 'All we still need to do is to include the stars.'

The night is dark and the stars are bright in the sky. Dave collects a book from the chalet and we spend an interesting hour identifying the most prominent star clusters and stars of the southern skies, such as:

## The Southern Cross

The southern cross consists of four stars in the format of a cross, plus a fifth smaller star roughly in the middle. To find true south, take the long leg of the cross, extend this length approximately four and a half times in the direction of the foot of the cross, and at this point drop vertically down to the horizon to find south. The southern cross is useful for survival not only on the seas but also in the wild.

## Three kings or Orion's belt

The three kings or the belt of the hunter, Orion, is another important and easily recognisable group. The three bright stars are accompanied to the side of the middle star by three smaller stars pointing away at about a 40 degree angle, the sword of the hunter. The position of three kings is right above the equator. When Orion appears in the evening, it indicates the position of true east and when Orion sets, true west.

## Milky way

On a dark night like tonight, the milky way stands out like a broad band of brilliant stars, stretching all the way from the southern cross right across the sky. Astronomers estimate between 100,000 and 400,000 million stars in the milky way, making us a very tiny part of our own galaxy indeed!

## The three brightest stars

Sirius, Canopus and Alpha Centauri

are the three brightest stars in the southern skies and therefore relatively easy to detect. To find Sirius, extend Orion's belt eastwards, straight to Sirius, the brightest star. The name, unsurprisingly means 'shiny one' or 'the bright one' and is a blue-white star, one of the closest to earth at only 8.5 light years away. During the 19th century Sirius intrigued astronomers as it seemed that the star was moving slightly. It turned out to be a relatively small but very heavy sister star which rotates around Sirius, causing the impression of movement from afar. Sirius is also known as the dog-star, being the principal star of the constellation of Canis Major.

Canopus, the second brightest star only displays about half the brightness of Sirius. Moving straight up from the Southern Cross, we come across Canopus. It is 650 light years away from earth and, had it been closer, would have been the brightest star as it is estimated to be 80,000 times as bright, as well as thousands of times as large as our sun, one of the yellow giants in the sky. It was even used as a space beacon for space craft launching, and guided the Mariner spacecraft around our planets.

The third brightest star and also the nearest to earth is Alpha Centauri. It is one of stars pointing from the horizon to the Southern Cross (the one nearest to the horizon) and is only 4.25 light years from earth. Like Sirius, Alpha Centauri is not only one star, but three, this time orbiting each other.

## Seven sisters (Pleiades)

There are of course many more constellations and stars to view, but the Pleiades or seven sisters is the last group of easily identifiable stars we have time to find. Looking again in line with Orion's belt, but this time in the opposite direction (west) to Sirius, we first notice the Hyades or letter A, a set of five stars, followed by a small cluster of stars called the seven sisters. According to astronomers this is one of the youngest clusters of stars visible from the earth, all young white or blue-white stars surrounded by gas and dust clouds which you find when stars are born. The name seven sisters is a misnomer. Looking through a telescope you can see many more than seven, and counting with the naked eye, you can only really see six! I wonder what happened to the seventh sister.

## Planets

When the night sky is dark it will be the stars that attract attention with their sparkling brightness. We have already noticed the even reflection of Venus as the evening star near the setting sun, and although not this time, most of us have seen the red colour of Mars in the sky. However without a telescope and a solar timetable to help us to find the planets, they have to wait for another evening.

*         *         *

It is with a feeling of sadness, but also fulfilment that we say goodnight for the last night together. Tomorrow we split up for the final stretch of the tour.

# 10. Karoo Plateau

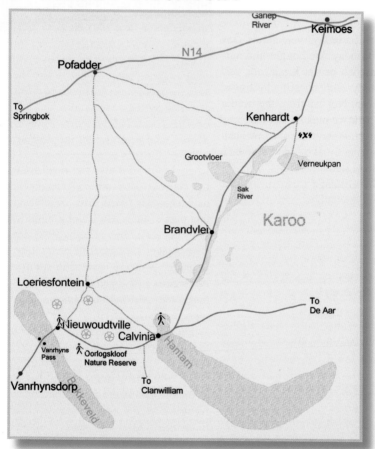

**Northern Cape Tourism Authority**
15 Dalham Road, Kimberley 8301
Tel: +27 (0)53 832 2657
Email: tourism@northerncape.org.za
Website: www.northerncape.org.za

**Namakwa Tourism Information**
Calvinia Museum, 44 Church Street
Private Bag X14, Calvinia 8190
Tel: +27 (0)27 341 8500
Email: tourismbk@namakwa-dm.co.za

**Green Kalahari Regional Tourism Office**
Private Bag X6039
c/o Hill and Le Roux Streets
Upington 8800
Tel: +27 (0)54 337 2800/26
Email: greenkal@bodr.gov.za
Website: www.greenkalahari.co.za

# 10. Karoo Plateau

*Above: A San roadside stall near Kgalagadi*

Today is Saturday, Valentine's Day and Paul's birthday. We bought him a T-shirt and baseball cap at Kgalagadi, and he immediately exchanges his borrowed hat for the cap. Not far from the border gate to the park we make a last stop at a roadside San craft stall to buy a few hand crafted souvenirs to take back home as a reminder of the memorable few days we have had the privilege to share in their country.

At Upington we say goodbye to Johan and Janey, who are heading back home to Noupoort, while we retrace our steps along the Gariep to Keimoes for the turn-off to Kenhardt. It takes four bridges to cross the river and on both sides we can see some of the 120 islands around Keimoes, all lush and green - a fitting farewell to the Green Karoo.

## Kenhardt

The road to Kenhardt brings us back to the Karoo plateau with its sparse vegetation and open spaces but this time to a place which, during the 19th century, became notorious as the Wild West of South Africa, a hiding place for cattle rustlers and outlaws from the Cape.

While it is not possible to pinpoint the exact origin of the name Kenhardt, the name had already been in use in 1863 when Louis Anthing, the magistrate of the Namaqualand region, recommended that a magisterial district be created in this part of the Cape Colony to curb the rampant lawlessness. He suggested that it should retain the name of Kenhardt, being 'a name which is generally known in these parts'. In December 1868 the new magistrate Maximilian Jackson arrived, with a group of fifty policemen, to suppress a Koranna uprising and to build the first police station and magistrate's office in Kenhardt. The camel thorn tree under which they first camped, has been acknowledged as the official birthplace of Kenhardt and has been declared a national monument. After this shaky beginning,

## Kenhardt
All business facilities
Hotel and guest houses

**Attractions:**
Quiver tree forest
Historical sites
Archeological sites
Verneukpan

*Above left: A phone number on the wall to help stranded tourists in Kenhardt*

*Above right: Quiver tree forest with Kenhardt in the background*

Kenhardt developed to become the most southern town in the Green Kalahari district of Kai !Garib and the capital of the dorper sheep farming region.

Rejoice! We found the solution to the tourist's nightmare of being stuck in a deserted remote town or village over a weekend. As we check in at the Kenhardt Hotel, the receptionist gives us the usual warning that we have to make sure to pick up the key to the locked gate of the nearby quiver tree forest from the information centre before they close at one o'clock for the weekend. A madly rushed few minutes later we arrive at the Information Centre with ten minutes to spare, and a locked door! This time, however there is a huge permanent message painted on the wall of the building giving a mobile phone number as contact in case the office is closed. I take them up on this promise and it works. I receive clear instructions of where to find the key, what to do in case it is not at its usual spot, and what to do when we leave the forest. Surely this is a method that can be adopted by many of

the remote locations to help them, as well as any frustrated tourist in need of some advice or assistance!

We spend some time in the quiver tree forest which is not so much a forest as collection of trees growing among the scattering of ironised rocks along a ridge outside Kenhardt. This is the first time on the tour that we have a chance to observe these desert members of the aloe family in bulk and take advantage of the chance for photographs.

Afterwards, Johanna and I stroll through the town to look at the other historical sites while Dave and Paul are having a rest before dinner. The camel thorn tree marking the birthplace of the town is not too far from the hotel. It dominates the surroundings and is marked by a plaque. Interesting too is the old library building which dates back to 1897 and which functioned as a library until 1977 when the library moved to the newly constructed municipal building opposite the street. We also pick up another link in the history of the Green Kalahari. The Dutch Reformed Mission Church on the southern outskirts of the town was built in 1896 and the first serving minister was the Reverend CWJ Schröder from Olyvenhoudtsdrift, Upington. He must have extended his reach southwards after Upington and Keimoes.

Although we do not have time to go on any of the available tours, there are two trips that I would have liked to have made from Kenhardt. The first is the 45 km drive to have a look at the seven toed footprints and San rock paintings. The footprints are large impressions of a round foot with seven toes, and are spaced approximately three metres apart. They are linked to a local Khoisan legend that this giant, half animal, half person, emerged from the soft rocks and terrorised the area. Following this, a visit to the farm Arbeidsvreugd, 60 km from Kenhardt will be a suitable encore, as there are remnants and paintings of a San colony who roamed this area. Their stories were told by //Kabbo, a member of the colony who was imprisoned in the Cape in 1870 and whose tales were recorded.

As the only residential guests in the hotel, the receptionist has given us the choice of having the usual hotel menu for dinner, or to join other dinner guests for the annual Valentine dinner and dance. We opt for the Valentine dinner. The hotel has put in a lot of effort to decorate the dining room in festive red and green and we are accompanied by what seems to be half the residents of Kenhardt for the three course meal and subsequent dance, quite a fun night to conclude the tour.

## Riverbeds and salt pans

It is in this part of the Karoo plateau that the dry river beds and salt pans speak of one-time abundance when the Karoo used to be an inland lake. The break-up of Gondwanaland 300 million years ago resulted in the folding and formation of the escarpment mountain ranges along

*Above left: Camel thorn tree as the birth place of Kenhardt. The church is in the background*

*Above right: Kenhardt's original library which served the community for 80 years*

the coastal belt of Southern Africa. Locked in by mountains of 2,000 m along the western coast and up to 4,000 m in the east, the Karoo and Kalahari plateaus became and internal lake at a height of around 1,000 m. Over the millennia, as the continent moved through tropical to desert conditions, the inland lakes on the plateau dried up, and left us with the 395,000 sq km dry plains of the Karoo. Even the name Karoo is derived from the Khoikhoi word Karusa, meaning 'dry barren thirst land'.

The longest of the dry river beds in the Karoo is the Sak River. The name sagging, could refer to fast disappearing water and its source is in the Nuweveld Mountains near Beaufort West in the middle of the Karoo. It ends in the dry lakes and salt pans north of Brandvlei, 450 km further on. This area between Calvinia and Kenhardt is covered by these salt pans. Although the largest pan is Grootvloer, aptly translating to large floor, north of Brandvlei, the most famous is Verneukpan to the east of Grootvloer.

## Verneukpan

Leaving Kenhardt, we have a choice of two roads to Brandvlei, or rather, one good tarred road and one very poor farm track which would take us to Brandvlei via Verneukpan, a salt pan approximately 20 km by 42 km in size, south-east of Kenhardt. The name Verneukpan, Afrikaans for pan of deception, comes from the illusion of water, created by mirages in the heat of the day. It is also the pan on which Sir Malcolm Campbell attempted a world land speed record in his Bluebird I in 1929. The track is still there, stretching a distance of 26 km in an easterly direction and quite a few stories still abound relating to this event:

How the pan lived up to its name in the misfortunes that Campbell's party had to endure, such as a plane crash near Calvinia, the temporary loss of his dispatch case with his papers, and his eventual failure to gain the world speed record,

How the locals helped to sweep the track before the event to get rid of stones, rocks, snakes and scorpions and fill in the holes where these were removed,

The festive mood as the date approached with news stands, flocking visitors, food stalls and camps,

How the preparation took longer than planned and the date had to be postponed so often that a tortoise found on the track was christened Bluebird II in the expectation that it might even turn out to be the eventual winner!

---

### Brandvlei
All business facilities
Hotel and guesthouses

**Attractions:**
Salt pans
Hiking

---

*Above left: A typical Karoo scene including a dust devil, the fond name for a small whirlwind*

*Above right: The Grootvloer salt pan between Kenhardt and Brandvlei*

Campbell reached a practice speed of 254 mph at Verneukpan, but his official run of 218.45 mph for the measured mile was not enough to break the world record of 231.36 mph. He did however succeed in setting a record for the five mile distance of 212 mph. Sir Malcolm Campbell eventually achieved his land speed record and exceeded speeds of more than 300 mph, not at Verneukpan, but on the Bonneville Salt Flats in Utah, USA in 1935.

Before we leave Kenhardt, the locals warn us not to attempt the detour to Verneukpan with only one car as the possibility of punctures is high and there are no reception towers for mobile phones along the way. The best alternatives would have been to join an organised tour where we could stay over on an adjoining farm, to travel in a 4x4, or else at least to travel in a group of two or more cars. We therefore stick to the easier, though no less interesting, tarred road to Brandvlei.

The dry Sak River spreads out into a series of salt pans all the way from north of Williston, around Brandvlei, to south of Kenhardt and we have to cross at least one of these enormous pans, Grootvloer. Although the landscape is already flat with low hardy shrubs, the pans are easily discernable. The surface of the pan has a cracked mud appearance, except that the mud is white brackish soil, interspersed with a few clumps of hardy grass. During the rainy season water may collect in the pans, turning them into oases for birds and popular venues for watching migratory birds.

## Brandvlei

Brandvlei, as mentioned, lies on the banks of the Sak River. For that matter, when the town received municipal status in 1961, a cynical view could have been that the river celebrated this event by flooding and splitting the town in two! The name Brandvlei may refer to one of the migrating farmers, named Brand, which is a common Afrikaans surname, and who stayed here for a while. Another source prefers to link the name to a specific fire which happened here, as the word brand is also Afrikaans for fire. The settlement developed in 1894 and today the town lies in the heart of a sheep and wool farming region, as well as having a thriving salt producing industry. One of the world's largest salt producers, Saltcor operates from here.

## The Hantam

As we approach Calvinia the scenery changes from the flat Karoo plains, to the dolerite topped mountains of the Hantam. Even though we all enjoyed the open vastness of the Karoo, we welcome the sight of the mountains of the escarpment.

The word Hantam refers to heyntame, a Khoikhoi name for 'the place where the red edible bulbs (Pelargonium bifolium, or uintjies in Afrikaans) grow'. Most of this mountain range is included and protected

---

**Calvinia**
All business facilities
Hotels, full range of accommodation

**Attractions:**
Historical buildings and sites
Museums
Giant post box
Akkerdam Nature Reserve
Vleisfees (meat festival)

---

by the Akkerdam Nature Reserve, 25,000 ha in size and four kilometres from the town of Calvinia. The park offers great hiking opportunities in the mountains. There is even a short two km walk for the elderly, which can be completed in one hour and is worth a go if you are short of time. The nearby Karee dam is a favourite stopover for migrating birds, and you may want to find out more or even help with the project to save the highly endangered riverine rabbit from extinction.

On the outskirts of Calvinia we stop at a service station and Mile 250, for fuel and a snack. It turns out to be a good choice. The tearoom is a cool, air conditioned room which not only caters for their human guests, but has a doggie menu on the wall with dishes like:

> meat with gravy
> chicken with gravy
> a bowl of milk
> water (free).

The attached shop also has a wide selection of home produce and crafts for sale, just right for the last minute presents before going back home.

## Calvinia

Calvinia was established in 1847 when the Dutch Reformed Church purchased a portion of a farm from Field Cornet A van Wyk for a new congregation. It was named Calvinia after the Swiss religious reformer Johannes Calvin. The

*Above top: Start of the Hantam range near Calvinia*

*Above: Original farmhouse, the Hantam House in Calvinia*

*Right: Giant post box in Calvinia*

town lies in the heart of the sheep and wool producing regions of the country, as demonstrated by the annual Hantam Vleisfees or meat festival, celebrated in August. The festivities start on the Friday with the usual floats and beauty pageants and continue with sporting events, food (very much mutton based) and craft stalls, sheep dog and other championships, dances and shows.

Our main stop in Calvinia actually covers three sites, namely the Dutch Reformed Church which towers stately over its neighbours, the Hantam House and the more recent addition of the giant post box. I want to start with this latest addition, as it demonstrates the ingenuity used by local towns in order to

promote themselves. Calvinia decided to camouflage its water tower, next to the Dutch Reformed Church by building a giant red pillar post box around it. It is a working post box and if you post letters in it, they will be dispatched with a special stamp! Luckily the actual slot is at the side as it is impossible to reach the top.

Opposite the post box is the Hantam House, the home of the original owner of the property. It was built in 1854 by Field Cornet A van Wyk, in the traditional gabled Cape Dutch style. The award winning building is a national monument, still with the original cedar wood panels. It also offers a tearoom and other delicacies to visitors. Another attraction is the museum in the old Synagogue dating

145

back to the 1920s, featuring the history of the area and quite a few other weird collections and displays like an ostrich chick with four legs.

The area around Calvinia was also the setting of more sinister events in the distant as well as the more recent past. General Smuts and his commandos were active around Calvinia during 1901 and the early part of 1902. From here they could conduct excursions towards Vanrhynsdorp and the coast until they moved northwards to the copper mountains near Springbok. You can follow the historic routes of the war, including the grave of Abraham Esau, who was tortured and executed for resisting the Boer commandos. His grave is just to the west of Calvinia and a memorial was erected 4 km to the east of the town near the spot where he was killed.

**Oorlogskloof** or war ravine, between Calvinia and Nieuwoudtville, on the other hand, has nothing to do with the Anglo Boer War. It was named after a much older war dating back to 1739 when serious skirmishes erupted between the migrating farmers and Khoikhoi tribes, after continuous incidents of cattle theft and counter-theft committed by both parties. One attack by government forces was against a settlement of Klaas Jantjie Klipheuwel, a Khoi chief in the ravine. Peace was established only after at least 13 members of the group were killed and sheep and cattle were confiscated. The ravine in which this settlement was situated was subsequently named Oorlogskloof.

The 4,770 ha Oorlogskloof Nature Reserve was established in 1983, funded by the World Wide Fund for Nature in South Africa, and the government conservation funds. The development of the reserve started in 1987 and the De Vondeling valley was added in 1990. The ravine is at the edge of the escarpment, and offers impressive though difficult hikes, mountain bike and 4x4 trails for the adventurous and nature lover. You can also visit glacial rock striations dating back to the Dwyka ice age era of around 280 million years ago, watching out for the booted eagle, black stork or other birds frequenting this area and increase your respect for nature.

---

**Nieuwoudtville**

All business facilities
Hotel and guesthouses

**Attractions:**
Bulbs and flowers in spring
Waterfall
Oorlogskloof Nature Reserve
Geological sites

---

## Nieuwoudtville

Nieuwoudtville is situated at the point where four ecosystems meet, namely the Hantam mountains, the cold Bokkeveld mountains, the flat open Nama Karoo and below the escarpment

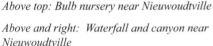

*Above top: Bulb nursery near Nieuwoudtville*

*Above and right:  Waterfall and canyon near Nieuwoudtville*

the unique Knersvlakte, each region with its own unique fauna and flora. But Nieuwoudtville is even better known as the bulb capital of the world with the highest concentration of indigenous wild bulbs growing and flowering from May to October.

The Glen Lyon Wild Flower Reserve on Neil McGregor' farm has managed to successfully combine sheep farming with the conservation of these wild bulbs. He hosted distinguished guests like Sir Ghilleam Prance from Kew Gardens in London and Sir David Attenborough, while filming part of his series on the 'Private World of Plants'. The variety of more than 300 of the Bulbinella species, including the famous indigenous red cat's tail (Bulbinella latifolia, var. doleritica) makes for a colourful and unforgettable display.

Approximately seven km north of the town is another landmark, the 100 metre waterfall in the Doring River, a great sight after winter rains and popular for watching raptors and other birds living in the reserve.

Nieuwoudtville was established in 1897 and named after the Nieuwoudt brothers on whose farm it was built. Today it is in the centre of a wheat, rooibos and honey tea (Cyclopia vogelii) area in addition to sheep farming for which this region is also suited. The honey coloured sandstone buildings offer a warm

*Right:  View over the Knersvlakte and Olifants River from Vanrhyns pass*

## Loeriesfontein
All business facilities

**Attractions:**
Flowers in spring
Museum
Quiver tree forest

welcome, and like all towns and villages along the western coast, Nieuwoudtville comes to life during the flower season in August and September.

## Loeriesfontein

About 65 km to the north of Nieuwoudtville is Loeriesfontein, another town in the heart of the sheep farming Nama Karoo. I could trace two origins to the name. The first, and most probably the more accurate explanation is that it was named after Lurie, a Jewish travelling salesman who frequented this area and used to stop over at the fountain. The other legend is that it was named after the song of the birds called loeries (Turacu corythaix) in Afrikaans, at the spring.

Loeriesfontein attractions include the museum in the old Baptist church, and a unique collection of wind pumps. Like Kenhardt it also has a Quiver tree forest outside the town.

## Vanrhyns pass

We started the tour at the foot of a pass, the Piekenierskloof pass. This was our entrance to the escarpment and coastal region of the north-western coast of South Africa, leading on to the plateau on top of this escarpment. It is therefore appropriate to end the tour on top of this plateau, looking down the escarpment from the look-out post at the top of the Vanrhyns pass between Nieuwoudtville and Vanrhynsdorp. Here we are literally standing on the edge of the world with a sheer drop below our feet and the Olifants River basin and Knersvlakte stretched out in front.

To the right you can see the white blotches of the pebbles on the Knersvlakte. To the left is the Matzikamma range and the Olifants River along the foot of the mountains towards the sea. In the distance we can see the mist clouds over the Atlantic at Strandfontein. We have arrived back at the Olifants River where we started from, the end of our journey of discovery.

\*     \*     \*     \*

During our last night together in Kgalagadi I asked the members of the group the key question:

'What part of the tour made the biggest impression on you?'

Paul liked everything, but especially the game viewing in the Kgalagadi Transfrontier Park. He went further to isolate the days when we saw the lions and then the ostrich families as special days.

Janey had a few outstanding days. The first one was the visit to Port Nolloth, the surprise of the town after all the negative comments in travel guides, and then watching the boats returning in the evening mist. Her other favourites were the hike between Strandfontein and Doring Bay and the visit to the succulent nursery at Vanrhynsdorp. These were closely followed by animals in Kgalagadi, but this time the ground squirrels in the camps!

Johan enjoyed the hike to Doring Bay, but also the evening tour through the Kgalagadi Park at Nossob, and the opportunity to see nocturnal animals which are otherwise invisible to visitors.

Johanna especially liked the inclusion of historical sites and the history of the places we visited, such as the visit to Darter's grave, Bowesdorp and Pella.

Dave enjoyed the sounds of silence of the open spaces, the pools at Augrabies, Twee Rivieren and Le Must to cool off after hot drives, and the luxury and peacefulness of the garden and setting of Le Must, where he could relax.

I personally enjoyed the continuous changing scenery and the beauty of each region. I also liked the history, and the research that was necessary to gather the information and try to distil the facts from fiction or myth.

We have learnt a few lessons that can help future tours like this, and spell them out in the final chapter of the book, but after balancing all the factors, it was a memorable and worth while experience.

The three of us who were born in Namaqualand, can now say: 'We know this part of the country really well for the first time'.

Our partners can say: 'We understand better and can appreciate more'.

# Then came the Rain

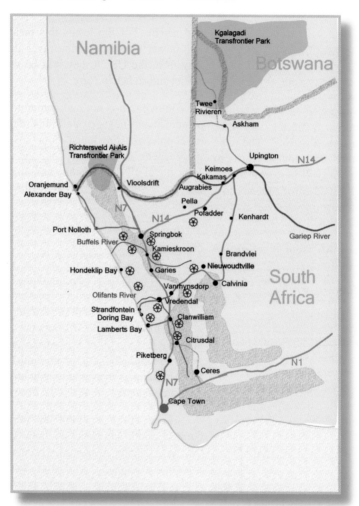

**Northern Cape Tourism Authority**
15 Dalham Road, Kimberley 8301
Tel: +27 (0)53 832 2657
Email: tourism@northerncape.org.za
Website: www.northerncape.org.za

**West Coast Regional Tourism
Organisation**
PO Box 242, Moorreesburg 7310
Tel: +27 (0)22 433 2380
Email: tourism@capewestcoast.org
Website: www.capewestcoast.org

# Then came the Rain

## Local knowledge

2001 was an excellent year for flowers in Namaqualand. In contrast, for the first time in living memory there were no flowers at all in 2003. The rains came too late and not enough. How can you know that you will be lucky before committing your hard earned money to a holiday from abroad or the more remote parts of South Africa?

'For a good flower year, the first rains should arrive during April and from then on at least once every two to three weeks to the end of July,' is the advice of the knowledgeable locals.

Although we conscientiously phoned Johanna every three weeks from April, it was only by the end of July that she told us that there will be flowers, but that they will be late - September rather than August, and that the displays will be thin

*Above: Yellow daisies reclaiming farm land near Nieuwoudtville*

and patchy. For the locals this means a non-flower year, but if you travel all the way from the UK, it may still be worth while, and so here we are.

But why? It is not uncommon to see meadows and fields of daffodils, daisies or poppies, or the forest floor covered in bluebells or snowdrops in the UK. Why travel all this distance and at great expense to see the same, only in different colours?

It is because you don't expect to see this abundance in a drought stricken area. The flowers are not predictable. The good sites this year may have nothing next year. It all depends where the strips of rain fall. Part of the fun and excitement is to find out where the flowers are best, not only this year, but this week, and to travel through the dry shrub-land until the bushes turn green, and then to see the burst of colour as you reach the flowers.

Flower displays along the western coast of South Africa are of three types: the mass display of daisies who are the pioneers in trying to reclaim disused land; the nurtured flower reserves; and the wild flowers, celebrating life wherever and whenever they can. Visit Namaqualand during the flower season with these intentions and you will not be disappointed. All the information centres will have the latest directions to the best flowers sites in the immediate surroundings for your enjoyment.

151

## Pioneer plants

The first time I heard the phrase 'pioneer plants' coined by the reverend Engelbrecht, it quelled a nagging doubt in my mind. For years I have been concerned about the fuss made over the large displays of Namaqua daisies on postcards and advertisements. Surely these are only farmers sowing the seeds in their unused agricultural land to attract visitors at a fee!

The truth is that even though there may be parts where this is done, the reality lies in the fact that the flower seed is the first to settle in unused agricultural fields which were initially cleared to grow wheat in a region totally unsuitable for agriculture, and then abandoned when the rains stayed away.

The flowers are only trying to reclaim the land for nature against all odds.

*Right: A field of daisies near Nieuwoudtville*

*Left: A display of purple vygies on a deserted farm yard near Doring Bay*

*Right: Yellow and orange daisies, tall yellow cat's tail and other flowers in the yard of a house in Nieuwoudtville*

*Right: Flowers in the Succulent Nursery near Vanrhynsdorp*

*Below: Ramskop Nature Reserve at Clanwilliam*

*Below left and right: Skilpad Flower Reserve near Kamieskroon*

## *Nurtured existence*

However there are nature reserves where the flowers are encouraged and re-seeded and if possible even watered each year to ensure good displays. Nothing wrong with this. We need flower reserves like Ramskop at Clanwilliam, Hester Malan outside Springbok and of course the well-known Skilpad Flower Reserve near Kamieskroon, developed by the WWF of South Africa. At least the visitor or locals, unable to travel to the wild sites, can enjoy these guarded displays.

## Wild abandon

But now we come to my personal favourite. Although the displays may be less dramatic I prefer to find and revel in the flowers among the natural shrubs and bushes. Unhindered by man the seed was lying dormant, only to germinate when the time is right. This is when you can look at mass displays, but also at the small detail of variety.

*Left: No patch without flowers, near Lamberts Bay*

*Below: Cotton bush in flower near Vanrhynsdorp*

*Above: Orange and white daisies on a farm near Graafwater*

*Right: Milkbush in flower near Vanrhynsdorp*

## *How many kinds*

I remember when as a child our school held a competition whereby the children were encouraged to make a scrap book of all the different flowers they could find during spring. I managed around 30 distinctly different kinds, but the winner collected more than 120! It gives as much pleasure to view the variety than the collective beauty.

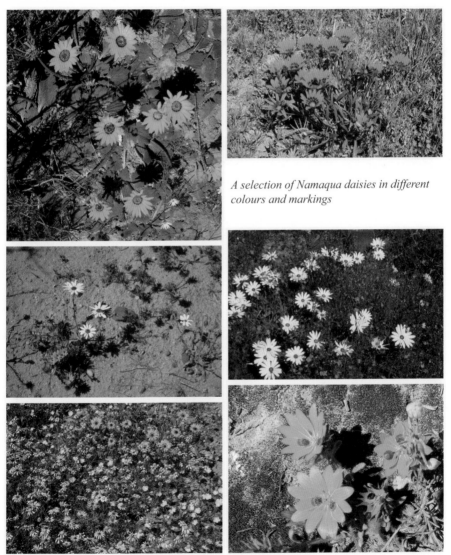

*A selection of Namaqua daisies in different colours and markings*

*Bulbs of all kinds flowering in the wild*

*The rich colours and varieties of vygies*

*Do look closely and you will dis-cover flowers in miniature*

# Practical Touring

All the arrangements for the tour in this book were made by members of the group, over the internet, by phone or by fax. Although some of the internet websites for the smaller towns and hotels were still very basic, additional phone calls soon sorted out queries or concerns. We travelled in two cars and took necessary precautions when travelling on dirt roads. We experienced no problems and found everyone we met very friendly and helpful.

The aim of this chapter is to provide some hints and tips which can help visitors to ensure a pleasant visit to this fascinating area.

## Accommodation

Although accommodation can be obtained all along the route, the following pointers may reduce disappointment and increase the level of enjoyment.

Book your accommodation at the start of your trip, or at least before you arrive at a town or village. During the flower season you are unlikely to find free rooms if you arrive unannounced, and during the quiet time of the year most guest houses and even hotels in the small villages are either closed or scaled down. By booking in advance it will give the proprietors a chance to prepare the rooms and ensure a pleasant stay. Accommodation in some of the more remote villages and towns is basic and caters mostly for local rather than overseas tourists, but they will go out of their way to accommodate your wishes.

Parks Board accommodation is good, usually including air cooling systems for the hot summers and are built for outdoor living.

If you are after luxury, you may have to limit your accommodation to either the well-known business/tourist hotels in the larger towns, or go to the luxury private game and leisure farms. These are readily available around and south of Vredendal, around the Green Kalahari and the game reserves. In between you may find the choice more restrictive.

Good publications are available on accommodation at local bookstores, information centres or on the internet. You can also find, and often book, your accommodation on the internet by checking hotel chain websites, or the local town or district websites

## Business Hours

Nearly all businesses and shops close from 1 pm on a Saturday to 9 am on a Monday, except for the some cafés that may remain open during the weekend. Unless you have your own itinerary planned for the weekend, or know people to visit in the town or village, you may find it very lonely on your own.

Most businesses will also close for lunch between one and two pm each day. This trend is not generally adhered to in the larger towns like Vredendal, Springbok or Upington where you may find more shops open over the weekend and businesses during the lunch hour.

Banks follow normal business hours. You will be able to find cashpoints in the larger towns where you can use international facilities like Switch, but this may be a problem in the smaller villages. It is better to make sure that you have enough cash for your needs, a credit card may not always be acceptable.

## Climate

Along the coast the temperature retains a pleasant range between 18 and 25 degrees Centigrade throughout the year, although this is often accompanied by a cooler heavy fog, especially early morning and again later in the afternoon.

Inland, along the escarpment, in the Nama Karoo and Kalahari, the best time of the year to go will be autumn (April and May) or spring (August to October). The summer temperatures can rise to 45 degrees Centigrade in summer while the winter temperatures, especially at night, is likely to fall below zero. Remember that the houses in South Africa are designed to stay cool in summer, rather than to retain

heat in winter. Summer heat is however not accompanied by high humidity, and therefore more bearable, as long as you cover up from the direct mid-day sun to prevent sunstroke.

## Communications

Landline telephonic communication is available in all villages and on most farms in the region. Reception towers for mobile or cell phones can be found around towns, leaving large parts of the region, especially along the minor roads, without reception. For this reason it is important that you do not attempt to travel on remote deserted roads on your own, without informing someone of your destination and when you are expecting to arrive. This way you can be reached in case of emergencies.

Email and internet cafes are available in all the larger towns, some hotels and luxury guest farms.

## Currency and Payments

The South African currency is the Rand and prices are inclusive of VAT. Although all businesses in the larger towns and most of the hotels will accept common credit cards, it is worth while checking before purchasing items whether the shops in the smaller villages or the smaller guesthouses will accept the cards.

Take enough cash along for emergencies when leaving the larger towns.

## Customs and regulation

There are strict laws and regulations against the picking and transporting of plants or animals in the wild. Succulents and flower seeds can be purchased from registered nurseries and have to be accompanied by valid permits for their transportation. However if you travel abroad, there may still be the problem of taking these plants or seeds through your own custom areas. It is better to leave with only your memories and photos of your visits.

## Driver's guide

Tarred roads in South Africa are generally excellent and well maintained. The surface of untarred roads will depend on when they were last graded. You may be fortunate to be following a grader, in which case the surface will be good, or precede the grader in which case the surface could be corrugated with potholes. In this case, or where there are sandy roads, it is very important to reduce the tyre pressure of your car to allow a better grip on the surface. Speeding on a corrugated or sandy surface with high pressure tyres can be as dangerous as driving on ice. This is also the reason why the insurance on rental cars can be high for overseas visitors.

Car rental price for 4x4 vehicles is high, but if you plan to travel to some of the more remote regions or follow some of the 4x4 trails, it is the best choice for a tour. All rental vehicles from reputable agencies are in good condition. Make sure that you understand all the features of the car before you leave the building. Security locks in the cars can be tricky to manage unless you know how.

Driving is on the left and there is a general speed limit of 120 km per hour except in the built up areas where the limit is reduced to 60 km per hour. Traffic police are very strict in maintaining speed restrictions.

## Electricity

Electricity is freely available in towns and most villages, and since the late 1990, also in many of the smaller settlements following the government initiative of affordable housing and services. Remote settlements, parks and farms may still rely on generators or gas.

## Health and emergencies

It is important to arrange for health insurance when travelling to these areas. No injections are required as there is no malaria or other tropical diseases, but a first aid kit and general medical supplies is essential, especially if you are travelling on the 4x4 trails. Good medical facilities are available in all larger towns and limited facilities in the smaller villages, at a reasonable cost. As the South African health care system is very much reliant on medical insurance, serious emergencies may turn out to be very expensive for foreigners if they don't have adequate travel insurance.

## Information Centres and websites

The Information Centres in the larger towns and villages are very good and the staff very helpful. You can find very useful maps and brochures about the area, although the directions on how to reach some of the tourist attractions are not always clearly spelled out.

Information Centres in the smaller and more remote towns and villages often only come to life during the flower season from July to September. During these months the centre becomes the hub for local industries, arts, crafts and information on local tours or routes. While this is also the fun time for tourists, you may find that during the rest of the year, the centre is either closed or moves to a different venue, often the local museum.

Information Centres in the Parks are excellent.

All the districts and larger towns have their own websites on the internet and it is worth while checking these sites before you go as they contain information on local businesses, accommodation, attractions, events and the history of the area. Information on the key contact centres and websites are included for each of the areas covered.

## Language

Most people in South Africa can at least understand English as the language is taught from the earliest years at school. The commonly spoken language along the north-western coast of South Africa is Afrikaans, although remote communities like Richtersveld and Mier near Kgalagadi still use the traditional Nama or San dialects.

## Nature Reserves, Parks

The South African Parks Board responsible for the management of most of the game parks, has always been effective in managing these parks and facilities. Accommodation is good. You can book in as a visitor, or become a partner which will allow you discount prices for your stay. Overseas visitors are expected to pay a small tax to help with the maintenance of the parks - a small price to pay for the pleasure you get from this.

New and private parks are continuously being developed and you should check on facilities before going there.

## Organised tours

Many local tours or tour guides are available from the towns and villages, as well as tours to the remote regions run by national tour companies. Check the travel and local websites for details or travel magazines such as Getaway, a South African travel publication, where many of these tours are listed.

## Safety and security

The north-western Cape is known for having the lowest crime rate in South Africa, although it is still prudent to follow the standard safety and security measures you would follow in any country, such as not to leave visible items in your car, lock doors, and be vigilant.

## Sport and leisure

All the towns and villages offer sport and leisure facilities. You may want to contact the local sport or golf clubs or find out about fishing if near a river, hiking trails, mountaineering, mountain biking or 4x4 trails. Towns and villages may have active hiking clubs, or it is usually possible to ask the information centres to arrange for guides to accompany you on hikes.

\*     \*     \*     \*

Check the local Information Centres or websites for further details. If in the smaller towns, the information centre is closed during the off-season periods, information can be obtained from the municipal office or local museum.

# Know your Afrikaans

Like the Dutch language, from which Afrikaans was derived, words are strung together to form a single concept. It is therefore better to know the meaning of the key words and work out the meaning of the composite word for yourself rather than to try and remember the meaning of each word you see. The following key words have been referred to in the book, either as parts of place names or local commonly used words.

A key to the pronunciation is given below.

| Pronunciation | | ch | loch | ng | sing | v | visit |
|---|---|---|---|---|---|---|---|
| a | car | e | hen | o | fort | w | warm |
| ah | **ah** (long) | ee | deer | oo | boot | y | why |
| ai | hair | ew | yew | ooe | doer | y̲ | you |
| au | cause | f | fun | oy | boy | | |
| ay | play | i | sick | r | strong roll | | |
| c | corn | î | sit | u | cup | | |

**Baba** (ba'ba): baby. Used in the descriptive name of the succulent bababoudjies (babies' bottoms).

**Baklei** (ba'clay): to fight. The old Dutch spelling is used in the farm name Bakkely Plaatz (fighting place).

**Bees** (bees): ox. Used in the succulent beeskloutjie (the hoof of an ox).

**Berg** (berch): mountain. Widely found as integral part of the names of mountains.

**Beskuit** (bîs'cayt): rusk.

**Biltong** (bîl'tong): dried strips of salted meat.

**Bokkoms** (boc'coms): dried and heavily salted herring.

**Bok** (boc): goat. Used in Bokvasmaak (tether the goat).

**Boom** (booem): tree. This word is found in many local names of trees such as botterboom (butter tree) or kokerboom (quiver tree).

**Bos** (bos): bush or shrub.

**Braai** (bry): barbecue.

**Brak** (brac): saline or brackish water. Usually used in the name of river or fountain as in Brakrivier (brackish river) or Brakfontein (brackish fountain).

**Brandewyn** (bran'dî'vayn): brandy.

**Bredie** (bree'di): stew.

**Dassie** (das'si): rock rabbit.

**Die** (di): the. Most often used when it forms part of a name such as Die Eiland (the island) or Die Kneg (the servant).

**Doring** (dooe'rîng): thorn. Mostly used as part of the name of a tree, river or bay, as doringboom (thorny tree) or Doring (thorn) Bay.

**Drif(t)** (drîf): low water river crossing. The first part of the name will usually denote some event or characteristic peculiar to the spot such as Sendelingsdrift (missionary crossing) or Sanddrift (sandy crossing).

**Droog or droë** (drooech or drooe): dry. Used as a noun or pronoun as in droë rivier (dry river) or droë wors (dried sausage).

**Dwars** (dwars): skew or slanted. Used in names like Dwarsrivier (skewed river).

**Eiland** (ay'land): island.

**Fees** (fees): festival. Usually accompanied by a word describing the type of festival.

**Fontein** (fon'tayn): fountain.

**Fyn** (fayn): fine or delicate. Used as part of the biome name of fynbos (fine bush) in the Cederberg and Cape mountains.

**Gat** (chat): hole. Used in names such as Wondergat (wonder hole).

**Gif** (chîf): poison. Used in the name Gifberg (poisonous mountain).

**Goeie (chooey)**: good. Goede is the Dutch spelling used as part of historical names such as Goede Hoop (good hope).

**Groot** (chrooet): large. Used as descriptive part of names such as Groot Kolk (large whirlpool) or Grootvlei (large valley).

**Grotte** (chrot'tî): caves. Used in the names of caves like Stadsaalgrotte (city hall caves).

**Halfmens** (half'mens): half human. The specific name of one of the aloe variety of trees in the Richtersveld.

**Heks** (hex): witch. Used as part of names of farms or rivers such as Heksrivier (witch river).

**Heuning** (hew'nîng): honey. Used on its own or as part of names like Heuningvlei (honey valley).

**Hoek** (hooc): corner. Used in names such as Wildeperdehoek (wild horses corner) or Windhoek (windy corner).

**Hond** (hond): dog. Used in the name of Hondeklip (dog stone) Bay.

**Huis** (hays): house.

**Kanniedood** (can'ni'dooed): cannot die. This is the name of one of the succulents found in the Knersvlakte.

**Karringmelk** (car'rîng'melc): buttermilk. Used with beskuit to identify a specific popular flavour of rusk.

**Kind** (cînd): child. Used in Kinderlê (children lying here).

**Klawer** (clah'vîr): clover.

**Klein** (clayn): small. Used in names like Kleinzee (small sea).

**Klip** (clip): stone. Widely used as part of names like Hondeklip (dog stone) Bay, Kliphuis (stone house) or Letterklip (letter stone).

**Kloof** (clooef): ravine. Used in names like Piekenierskloof (ravine of the pikemen) or Oorlogskloof (war ravine).

**Kners** (cners): crunching or gnashing. Used to describe Knersvlakte (crunching plain).

**Koek** (cook): cake. Used singly or to describe a certain kind of cake like koeksisters (cake sisters) or skuinskoek (angular cake).

**Koker** (cooe'cer): quiver. Used as the Afrikaans name of the quiver tree because of the shape of the tree and leaves.

**Kop** (cop): head. Used in names like Ramskop (ram's head) or Spitskop (pointy head).

**Kos** (cos): food.

**Kuier** (cay'îr): visit. Referred to in kuierfees thereby describing the festival.

**Lekker** (leck'îr): nice or tasty. The name Lekkersing describes the joy of singing.

**Matjie** (mat'yi): little woven mat. Used in matjieshuis (reed mat house).

**Meerkat** (meer'cat): suricat. More commonly known by its Afrikaans name.

**Melk** (melc): milk. Widely used as part of names such as Melkboschkuil (milk bush pool) or melkkos (milk food).

**Messel** (mes'sle): bricklaying or masonry. Used in Messelpad (built-up road). Parts of the road were built by stonemasons.

**Mier** (mir): ant.

**Mis** (mîs): dung. As in misvloer (dung floor).

**Neus** (news): nose.

**Oestyd** (oos'tayd): harvesting time.

**Oorlog** (ooer'loch): war. As it was used in Oorlogskloof (war ravine).

**Pakhuis** (puck'hays): store room.

**Piekenier** (pic'e'nir): pikeman. Used in Piekenierskloof (ravine of the pikemen).

**Ratel** (rah'tîl): rattle. Usually referring to the rattle snake. Used in Ratelgat (rattle hole).

**Riem** (rim): strap. Used in the name Riemvasmaak (tie the strap).

**Riet** (rit): reed. Used in names like Rietmond (reed mouth), Rietpoort (reed gully).

**Rittel** (rît'tle): jive. As used in Rittelfees (jive festival).

**Rob** (rob): seal. Used in place names like Robbebaai (seal bay) or Robberg (seal mountain).

**Rooi** (rooey): red. Used in rooibos (red bush).

**Rooster** (rooes'ter): gridiron used in barbecues. Used to name roosterkoek (griddle cake).

**Saaityd** (sy'tayd): sowing time.

**Sak** (sac): sack or sagging. As used in Sakrivier (fast dropping water).

**Sand** (sand): sandy. Used widely to describe the nature of the place such as Sanddrif (sandy crossing), Sandveld (sandy veld).

**Sendeling** (sen'd î'lîng): missionary. Used in

Sendelingsdrift (missionary crossing).

**Skilpad** (scîl'pad): tortoise.

**Soebat** (soo'bat): to plead. Used in the name Soebatsfontein (pleading fountain).

**Spektakel** (spec'ta'cle): spectacular. Used in Spektakelpas (spectacular pass).

**Spruit** (sprayt): small stream. Used in the name Spruitdrift (small stream crossing).

**Stadsaal** (stad'sahl): town hall. Used in Stadsaalgrotte (town hall caves).

**Swart** (swart): black. Used in the name Swartdoring (black thorn) River or the Swartland (black country).

**Vasmaak** (fas'mahc): to tie or fasten. Used in Bokvasmaak (tie the goat).

**Velskoene** (fel'scoo'nî): leather shoes. The brand name for the typical shoes made in the Cederberg area.

**Vergenoeg** (fer'che'nooch): far enough.

**Viool** (fi'ooel): violin. Used in the name Vioolsdrif (violin crossing).

**Viswater** (fîs'vah'ter): fish water.

**Vlakte** (flac'tî): open plains. Used in Knersvlakte (crunching plains).

**Vlermuis** (fler'mays): bat. Used in Vlermuisklip (bat rock) or the old Dutch spelling of Fleermuijsklip.

**Vrede** (free'dî): peace. Used in the name Vredendal (peace valley).

**Vygie** (fay'chî): local name for the flowering succulent plant.

**Wit** (vît): white. Used in names like witblits (white lightning) or Witdraai (white corner).

**Wors** (vors): sausage. Most often heard as boerewors (farmer's sausage).

# JNDEX

# Bibliography

Allan, David: *First Field Guide to Birds of Prey of Southern Africa*, Struik Publishers (Pty) Ltd, Cape Town, 1999

Broodryk, Maritz: *Van Waterdrinkplek tot Vakansieoord. Die Geskiedenis van Strandfontein*, Lambertsbaai Drukkers, 1995

Bundy, C and C Saunders (cons.): *Illustrated History of South Africa - The Real Story*, Reader's Digest

Burger, CR: *Die Kamiesberg*, Geborg deur Die Namakwalandse Diamandfondstrust, Wimpy, Springbok en South African National Parks

Burman, Jose: *So High the Road*, Human & Rousseau (Pty) Ltd, Cape Town, 1963

Conradie, Franz: *Stargazing for the Novice*, Kransberg Communications, Orania, 2002

De Villiers, SJA: *Kook en Geniet*, Kaap en Transvaal Drukkers Bpk, Kaapstad, 1972

Dreyer, Eerw. A: *Kerksoewenier van Namakwaland - 'n Tagtigjarige rekord - 1850 tot 1930*, Pro-Ecclesia Drukkery, Stellenbosch, 1930

Deacon, J: *Some views on Rock Paintings in the Cederberg*; The National Monuments Council, Cape Town, 1998

Duvenhage, C: *Boere-Lekkernye*, Central News Agency Beperk, Suid Afrika

Engelbrecht, Henriette: *Kgalagadi Transfrontier Park*; South African National Parks, printed by The Tourist Blueprint, 2003

Hall, Hazel: *Taking the Waters - The History of The Olifants River Warm Baths*, Hazel Hall, The Baths (Pty) Ltd, Citrusdal, 2003

Hanekom, Dr. TN: *Die Gemeente Namakwaland, 'n Eeufees-Gedenkboek (1850 - 1950)*, NG Kerkpers, Woodstock, Kaap, 1950

Hattingh, GG: *Die NG Gemeente van Vredendal 25 Jaar Oud 1933 - 1958*; Die Kerkraad, Vredendal, 1958

Hoërskool Namakwaland: *Namakwalandse Resepte - Beproefde Versamelde Resepte*, Van's Photos, Springbok

Impson, ND, IR Bills and JA Cambray: *State of Biodiversity: Western Cape Province, South Africa Freshwater Fishes*, Western Cape Nature Conservation Board, Stellenbosch, 2000

Kotzé, Gert: *Die Anglo-Boereoorlog in Namakwaland*, Springbok Lodge & Restaurant, Springbok, 1999

Laerskool Spruitdrift: *Feesblad 1904 - 1979*, Protea Drukkery, Vredendal, 1979

Leipoldt, C. Louis: *Leipoldt's Cape Cookery*, WJ Flesch & Partners, Cape Town, 1983

Lions Club, Vredendal: *Vredendal*, 1983

Livingstone, David: *Missionary Travels in South Africa, Volume 1*, The Narrative Press, Santa Barbara, California, 2001

Manning, John: *First Field Guide to Succulents of Southern Africa*, Struik Publishers (Pty) Ltd, Cape Town, 2001

Manning, John: *First Field Guide to Wild Flowers of Southern Africa*, Struik Publishers (Pty) Ltd, Cape Town, 1999

Maritz, Manie: *My Lewe en Strewe*; Gen. M Maritz, Pretoria, 1939

Namakwalandse Streeksontwikkelings-vereniging: *Namakwaland*, ABC Pers (Edms) Bpk, Kaapstad, 1965

Oberholzer, I (ed.): *Namaqualand*, Protea Drukkery, Vredendal, 1984

Pakenham, Thomas: *The Boer War*, Abacus, London, 2000

Parker, Pippa (ed.): *Beautiful Birds of Southern Africa*, Struik Publishers (Pty) Ltd, Cape Town, 1994

Rosenthal, Eric (ed.): *Encyclopaedia of Southern Africa*, Frederick Warne & Co. Ltd, London, 1961

Schirmer, Peter: *The Concise Illustrated South African Encyclopaedia*, Central News Agency (Pty) Ltd, 1981

Schoeman, PJ: *Jagters van die Woestynland*, Nasionale Boekhandel Beperk, Kaapstad

Sinclair, Ian: *Field Guide to the Birds of Southern Africa*, C Struik (Pty) Ltd., Cape Town, 1984

Slingsby, P & E Coombe: *Beyond the Cederberg, Agter-Pakhuis, Biedouw, Wupperthal*, Baardskeerder, Muizenberg, 2001

Springbok Lodge & Restaurant: *Places worth visiting in Namaqualand*, Van's Photos, Springbok, 1998

Thristland Epic: *Heroic Struggle of Pioneer Missionaries in Namaqualand*, Trans-Oranje Drukkers, Upington,

Trew, Peter: *The Boer War Generals*, Jonathan Ball Publishers (Pty) Ltd, Jeppestown, 1999

Van der Merwe, SW: *Cederberg-Wildernisgebied*, 1993

Van der Post, Laurens: *The Lost World of the Kalahari*, Penguin Books Ltd, London, 1958

Van der Walt, Pieter: *Augrabies Splendour, A guide to the natural history of the Augrabies Falls National Park and the Riemvasmaak wildlife area*, CPD, 2000

Van Lill, Gert: *Vredendal 1944 - 1994*, Nasionale Boekdrukkery, Goodwood, Cape, 1994

Van Zyl, Ds. MJN (ed): *Hartland van God se veldblommetuin, Garies Eeufeesbundel 1904 - 2004*, Ned. Geref. Gemeente, Garies, 2004

## *Information Centres and Websites consulted:*

www.bushmanland.co.za
www.capenature.org.za
www.capetourism.org
www.capewestcoast.org
www.cederberg.co.za
www.citrusdal.info
www.clanwilliam.info

# BIBLIOGRAPHY

www.game-reserve.com
www.greenkalahari.co.za
www.northerncape.org.za
www.okiep.co.za
www.sanparks.org
www.thebaths.co.za

## Travel websites:

www.accommodationsouthernafrica.com
www.africa4u.co.za
www.african-expeditions.com
www.bushmanskloof.co.za
www.getawaytoafrica.com
www.go2africa.com
www.kaggakamma.co.za
www.kalaharigateway.co.za
www.places.co.za
www.southafrica-travel.net
www.thompsons.co.za
www.toursaa.com
www.witsandkalahari.co.za

## Historical/Information websites:

www.airports.co.za
www.cllp.uct.ac.za Living Landscape Project
www.conservation.state.mo.us Looking at Lichens
www.cwmission.org.uk Council for World Mission
www.kwv-international.com
www.mundus.ac.uk London Missionary Society
www.museumsnc.co.za
www.newadvent.org Catholic Encyclopaedia
www.online-literature.com The Great Boer War by Arthur Conan Doyle
www.rapidttp.com South African Military History – Anglo-Boer War
www.rbgkew.org.uk Royal Botanic Gardens, Kew
www.standardbank.co.za Cover of business facilities

## My personal thanks to:

Co-travellers Janey van der Merwe, Johanna van Zyl, Dave Dean, Paul Dean and Johan van der Merwe, for their enthusiasm and continued assistance. Also to my family Dave, Jennifer and William for their help and encouragement.

The professional and generous help from members of all the Tourist Information Centres. Ds. Hans Engelbrecht, Valerie Mentoor, Engela and Ena van Zyl and other friends along the way for sharing their personal experiences and historical knowledge. Roy and Carol Hill for 'test-driving' sections of the book and sharing their findings.

*Disclaimer: The maps in the book are not drawn to scale but for illustrative purposes only. Due care was taken to ensure the accuracy of the information, but travellers should contact the local Information Centres for accurate maps and up to date information.*

# Local Government Structure for towns visited

## Western Cape Province

### West Coast District

**Cederberg Municipality**

Citrusdal
Clanwilliam
Graafwater
Lamberts Bay

**Matzikama Municipality**

Vredendal
Vanrhynsdorp
Klawer
Lutzville
Ebenhaezer
Doring Bay
Strandfontein

**West Coast Municipality**

Bitterfontein
Nuwerus
Rietpoort

**Other Municipalities**

## Northern Cape Province

### Namakwa District

**Kamiesberg Municipality**

Garies
Kamieskroon
Hondeklip Bay
Kharkams
Leliefontein

**Nama Khoi Municipality**

Springbok
Okiep
Nababeep
Concordia
Steinkopf
Komaggas

**Richtersveld Municipality**

Port Nolloth
Alexander Bay
Richtersveld
villages

**Khai-Ma Municipality**

Pofadder
Aggeneys
Pella

**Hantam Municipality**

Calvinia
Brandvlei
Nieuwoudtville
Loeriesfontein

### Siyanda District

**Kai !Garib Municipality**

Kakamas
Keimoes
Kenhardt

**//Khara Hais Municipality**

Upington

**Mier Municipality**

Mier

**Other Municipalities**

### Kgalagadi District

Published by:

Dean & Associates Ltd,

16 Swallow Dale, Thringstone, Coalville, Leicestershire LE67 8LY England

Tel/Fax: +44 (0)1530 222 799   email: DeanAssocsLtd@aol.com


ISBN  0-9550228-0-0

British Library Cataloguing in Publication Data:

A catalogue record for this book is available from the British Library


**Print:**  CPD Ltd, Pretoria, South Africa

**Cartography and Design:**  CM Dean

**Photography:**  Members of the Dean and van der Merwe families

Cover illustrations:

**Front Cover:**  Quiver tree forest near Kenhardt

**Back Cover:**  Church at Pella;  Springbok in the Kgalagadi Transfrontier Park;  The road leading into Port Nolloth